Criticisms on the Bar
by John Payne Collier

Address:
HardPress
8345 NW 66TH ST #2561
MIAMI FL 33166-2626
USA
Email: info@hardpress.net

CRITICISMS UPON THE BAR

CRITICISMS ON THE BAR;

INCLUDING

STRICTURES

ON

THE PRINCIPAL COUNSEL

PRACTISING IN THE COURTS OF

KING's BENCH, COMMON PLEAS, CHANCERY, AND EXCHEQUER.

BY

AMICUS CURIÆ.

" I have done in this nothing unworthy of an honest life
" and studies well employed."

Milton. Pref. to Doctr. of Divorce.

LONDON :

PRINTED FOR W. SIMPKIN AND R. MARSHALL,
STATIONERS' COURT, LUDGATE STREET.

1819.

Printed by G. HAYDEN, Little College Street,
Westminster.

PREFACE.

WHEN the re-publication of these Cri
ticisms,* upon those who figure mos
successfully at the English Bar, was firs
proposed to me, I thought that it woul
not be amiss to introduce them by a sor
of preface, in justification of having
undertaken to write them at all. Upon
subsequent reflection, however, I hav
determined to abandon that design

* They were first printed in the Examiner in th
Autumn of 1818, except two, which have been adde
since

b

partly because it might be necessary to enter into circumstances now of little consequence to myself, and certainly of no importance to others—partly because it might impliedly cast a doubt upon the fairness of the attempt, and on the propriety of making it—but principally because I felt that nothing that could be urged would have the effect of convincing those who had made up their minds to the contrary.

It is but just that I should say that I have heard no objection seriously stated and argued to the fitness of subjecting Barristers to critical enquiry, but from Barristers themselves; and every one, who knows any thing of that body, must be aware, in the first place, that it

is extremely natural that they should b
averse to such discussions on their me
rits, defects, and qualifications; and i
the next, independent of their persona
reluctance, that there is no class of per
sons, from various causes, so difficult o
persuasion. Mandeville, in the prefac
to part II. of his FABLE OF THE BEES
observes, " I never think an author more
foolishly employed than when he is vin
dicating his own abilities ;" and I may
follow it up by saying, with reference
to what I have above remarked, that my
time could not be more fruitlessly oc
cupied than in endeavouring to satisfy
the subjects of these articles, and those
connected with them, that I had a right
thus to bring them before the public
This goes to the propriety of speaking

of them at all in print; the mode in which I have spoken of them must answer for itself.

Had I found that with those who are not Barristers any such notion had prevailed, as that while Actors, Artists, and Authors, are amenable to criticism, Barristers, (who stand pre-eminently forward as public characters, and live on the estimate which the world at large forms of their talents) ought to be exempted from it, I should have pursued a different course in this Preface, and should, perhaps, have troubled the Reader somewhat more at length. As it is, the few sentences with which I have closed the volume will, I apprehend, be sufficient.

PREFACE.

With regard to the particular conten of the volume it will be found that ind pendent of the addition of some ne pieces of criticism, not included in tl original series, various alterations an improvements have been made in almo every character; for wherever I foun reason to change the impression und which I first wrote, I have not scruple to state it, whether in favour or again the individual under observation. Son notes have also been appended to rend certain points more intelligible, as we as to communicate facts necessary to b known, and to mention events that hav occurred since the first appearance of th Article.

It will be seen that my strictures are confined to the Barristers practising in what are commonly termed the Courts of Westminster, including both Law and Equity:* I am aware that under the title of " Criticisms on the Bar" if I did not travel to Scotland or Ireland, it might be expected that I should have intro-

* I do not think that I have omitted to observe upon any of the King's Counsel whether of old or of recent standing, excepting Mr. Agar of the Court of Chancery. I do not know whether he will think any apology necessary; but the fact is, that I originally intended to have spoken of him with Messrs. Hart and Bell, but having neglected him then, I could not afterwards find a convenient place to include him. I may here take the opportunity of saying that his talents and knowledge are of no ordinary kind, and one reason for not criticising him at the same time with the gentlemen I have named, was, that I found that those two were tolerably equally matched, and that the mention of Mr. Agar would have disturbed the uniformity : certainly, in point of quickness, I should place him before them.

duced a specimen or two from the Con
sistory and Admiralty Courts. I admi
strictly speaking, that this is an omiss
on, but my knowledge of the individua
practising there was so general an
superficial that I did not feel warrante
in hazarding an opinion regarding th
mode in which they discharged the
duties. Drs. Lushington and Jenne
indeed, I have several times heard wit
much satisfaction, but if I had single
them out it might have appeared like a
invidious distinction, and would hav
given the reader but an imperfect notic
of their competitors. Besides, the mod
in which business is conducted in thos
Courts is so peculiar, and the tale
usually displayed so accommodated t

he situation, that my remarks, of course
always relative, must have been flat, and,
perhaps, unintelligible but to the very
few who are in the habit of attending
Doctors Commons.

When a re-publication was first suggested to me I wished to have added an
article more exclusively devoted to the
Junior Barristers, especially to such as
I think promise hereafter to distinguish
themselves. The names of several I have
lightly mentioned in different parts of
these Criticisms, when a reference to
them, for the sake of explanation or
illustration, was needed, and after some
consideration I determined, for many
reasons, not worth detailing, to forego

my design. I shall therefore leave thei
qualifications to be ascertained by som
future Critic, when they may hav
fulfilled the promise they at presen
hold out.

It may not be improper to subjoin
that if the period which has elapsec
since the first publication of these articles shall have injured the sale of the
volume, it has improved and matured it
contents, by giving me a longer time to
reflect upon the correctness or incorrect-
ness of the strictures I have made.

AMICUS CURIÆ

CONTENTS.

	Pa?
ON the Decline of Eloquence at the English Bar	
Mr. SCARLET	1
Mr. MARRYAT	2
Mr. Sergeant BEST	4
Sir SAMUEL SHEPPERD	6
Sir ARTHUR PIGGOT	7
Sir ROBERT GIFFORD	ç
Mr. TOPPING	1C
Mr. Sergeant LENS	12
Mr. Sergeant VAUGHAN	12
Mr. DAUNCEY	1ʒ
Mr. GURNEY	14
Mr. DENMAN	1ɛ
Mr. Sergeant COPLEY	1ʔ

	Page
Mr. JERVIS	191
Mr. RAINE	ibid
Sir SAMUEL ROMILLY	205
Mr. WETHERELL	221
Mr. Sergeant BOSANQUET	237
Mr. RICHARDSON	245
Mr. BROUGHAM	249
Mr. HART	265
Mr. BELL	ibid
Mr. NOLAN	275
Mr. GASELEE	278
Mr. CASBERD	280
Mr. WARREN	282
Mr. HARRISON	ibid
Mr. Sergeant PELL	287
Mr. CULLEN	297
Mr. HORNE	301
Mr. HEALD	303
Mr. WINGFIELD	304

CRITICISMS ON THE BAR.

Thou see'st thou neither are mark'd out nor named,
And therefore only to thyself art shamed ;
Now if thou stir'st at best thou shalt but make
The country of thy faults more knowledge take.
G. Wither's Abuses Stript and Whipt.

ON THE DECLINE OF ELOQUENCE AT THE ENGLISH BAR.

In commencing a series of critical article
upon the various qualifications of those wh
practise as Advocates in our Courts of Justice
it is far from my intention to controvert th
general opinion, that within the last 20, o
even within the last 10 years, the eloquenc
for which the English Bar was once so cele
brated has greatly declined : on the contrar

B

it is my wish in the outset to advert to a few of the causes which I think have led almost to its banishment.   Men who possess many of the most important requisites of accomplished orators are not wanting, nor are the occasions few on which they might display their powers. Among the younger members of the profession there are several of distinguished talents in this kind;   and from the seniors, bursts of energy and feeling are sometimes heard, and not unfrequently a very successful employ- ment of the better, or, at least, the more use- ful parts eloquence.   Compared however with a remoter period, the instances are rare, and serve principally to shew, that did Advocates yield more to their natural impulses, and less to the trammels by which circumstances have surrounded them, they might restore the Bar to something like the rank it formerly held in public estimation.

Fathers of families, and particularly those tolerably advanced in life, are often heard to assert, that the only profession in this country, where talents can insure success, is the Law.

If they mean talents of a popular kind—the power of giving effect to comprehensive views of justice and the bonds of society—a command of language, and a faculty of bringing to bear upon one point all the resources of intellect and knowledge, they are mistaken; they speak from former experience, not from present observation—from a recollection of what they have witnessed at an early age, without being aware, that since that time the employment of a Barrister has almost completely changed. They refer to the days of MINGAY and ERSKINE—not to those of MARRYAT and BELL;—to the time when Juries were wrought upon by the united influence of zeal and talent, not when they were governed by precedents and practice—when men were allowed to feel a little as well as to think a great deal, and were not required for ever to shut up their hearts in the dark recesses of their understandings.

With regard to the tedious and often unmeaning forms of law, there perhaps never was a time when the shrewd satire of RABE-

LAIS upon the proceedings of Courts of Justice could be better applied than at the present moment—all the learned arguments, all the citations from books, applicable and inapplicable—all the references to the *dicta*, and to the decisions of Judges, according to his humourous account, terminate but in the casting of a die; from which he intends it to be inferred, that while learning and industry are exhausted and wasted on the means, they are perfectly useless as to the end.＊   In making this reference, no imputation is of course intended to be cast upon the general decisions in our Courts : in indifferent causes, the determinations are indifferent ;   but justice would be quite as faithfully and much more speedily and effectually administered, if the greater part of the expensive forms, processes, and pleadings, so recently enlarged, if not

---

＊ Vide chap. 38, 39, and 40, of B. III. " Comment Bri
" doye expose les causes pourquoy il visitoit les proces
"＜ qu'il decidoit par le sort de dez," and " Comment Pan
" tagruel excuse Bridoye sus les jugemens faictz au sor
" des dez."—Edit. Paris, 1553. This and more from the
same book may be recommended to the perusal of al
young students.

introduced, and so carefully observed and
multiplied, were entirely disregarded :—it is
not too much to assert, that one fifth of the
causes that come before our Courts are de
cided upon mere matters of form, without the
slightest reference to the merits. So much
have they been augmented of late years, that
a new branch of the profession has actually
sprung out of them—the business of a *Special
Pleader* :—a young man who studies for the
Bar is now compelled to go through all the
complicated drudgery of the office of one o
these underlings* before he is qualified for
any higher walk :—all the knowledge he has
acquired, in twenty years at school and college, is thrown away; general principles and
enlarged notions of law and justice are smo-
thered in laborious and absurd technicalities
and the enervated mind becomes gradually
so accustomed to these shackles, that the en-
durance of them amounts to a habit; they
not only cease to seem burdensome, but cease

---

* Their business is called practising *under the Bar*
and two or three years are scarcely sufficient for the acquirement of the intricacies of this department.

:o be so; for instances are not unfrequent, where the natural vigour of the intellect has been so reduced as to make it even depend upon its bondage—as emaciated TRENCK is said at last to have received support from the very chains that fixed him to the walls of his dungeon.*

 A second cause, no doubt, is the vast accumulation of business within the last few years, which has necessarily compelled advocates, even of high talents and attainments, to be contented with the appellation of mere men of business : the number of actions tried

---

* Recollecting that three out of the four judges now presiding in the Court of King's Bench were distinguished as pleaders before their elevation, it is somewhat singular, but not the less satisfactory, to find, that in Hilary term 1819, soon after these articles were first published, a rule was made by their Lordships which lopped off many of the luxuriant excrescences of pleading, by limiting and restraining what are known as *sham-pleas* and *subtle-pleas*. From their early skill in framing them it is not unlikely that the three judges referred to were more sensible how they obstructed the real ends of justice, for the purpose of taking money out of the pockets of suitors, and putting it into those of attornies, special-pleaders, and counsel.

in the Court of King's Bench has of late nearly doubled, while, generally speaking, the management of them is entrusted to four King's Counsel, and to about twice as many assistants behind the Bar. At the last sittings at Guildhall* more than two hundred suits stood for decision, and the time that could be allowed for hearing the whole was at the utmost fifteen days; so that, as the Court usually sat for only six hours each day, supposing them all tried, there would be less than half an hour for the determination of each cause, a space much less than was formerly occupied by the opening speech of a Counsel. This calculation is however by no means fair, because, perhaps, not more than half, or at most two-thirds, of these actions came before a Jury. Besides, in the other Courts, and especially in the Common Pleas, the business has not increased in the same proportion.

But independently of these two considerations, which may perhaps be thought of comparatively minor importance, I do not

* July, 1818.

scruple to say, that the present dearth of eloquence at the English Bar is chiefly to be
attributed, on the one hand, to a depressing
spirit in the Court, and, on the other, to a
submissive spirit in the Council. "Pack-
bearing patience" is quite as indispensable a
requisite for a Barrister, if emolument be his
object, as a knowledge of the laws of his
country. Young men who start on their
career, who have just mounted their wig and
gown, of late years have obtained practice
not by any extraordinary display of the energies of mind or language in resisting oppression and vindicating those who have been
falsely accused, nor by an exhibition of penetration or acuteness in discovering and extracting truth from reluctant witnesses; but,
generally, by the publication of some treatise
upon a particular branch of the law, or by a
volume of reports of decided cases, accompanied by a fulsome dedication to an individual, who has the means of advancing them
in their progress by smiling upon their labours. This is what is termed "obtaining
the ear of the Court;" this is

———————— that trick of Courts to wear
Silk at the cost of flattery;

James Shirley's Poems.

for by such means not a few have risen to the
highest rank and highest emoluments of their
profession: prudent attornies are sure to employ those who are sure to be heard with
most indulgence. The undaunted and repeated refusal of ERSKINE to discontinue an
address he felt it his duty to make, when im-
periously commanded by a haughty Judge
to sit down, is not yet, and we hope will
never be, forgotten; it has illustrated him
and his successors more than the patrician
robes by which he has been since invested;
but let me ask, has it ever been imitated, or
who would have dared to imitate such a fear-
less discharge of duty had the necessity occurred? The blunt fortitude of honest JACK
LEE, (as he was familiarly called) and others
whom I could name, is also still remembered—but only remembered apparently to
be avoided.——It would be unfair, however,
not to allow that some part of the business-
like, mechanical mode, in which causes have

been recently conducted, is to be attributed to a reluctance on the part of the Court, that any imposition, or attempt at imposition, should be practised on the Jury.   The Lord CHIEF JUSTICE of the Court of King's Bench is a man of a strong and piercing intellect, and of uncommon powers of language; he often penetrates to the very bottom of a cause, when others, even the Council themselves, are only upon the surface.   His intuition in this respect is astonishing, and he cannot endure that valuable time should be wasted in endeavouring to deceive the good sense of a Jury, or on preliminary or immaterial points, while the true and only question is disregarded or forgotten.   This indeed is one source of the ordinary complaint against Lord ELLENBOROUGH (more especially by young Barristers) that he is hasty and severe—that he will not listen with becoming patience and forbearance : he certainly often will not : it is however but doing his Lordship justice to add, that in many cases those who are forcing themselves upon his attention have no right to complain of more than perhaps a needless degree of rudeness, in the manner in which they are interrupted or repulsed. I am no admirer of the general deportment of Lord ELLENBOROUGH, either on or off the Bench; but it is not unfrequently a very useful lesson and a very fine display of power, to witness the manner in which he drives directly onward to the just end of a cause—like a mighty elephant in a forest, trampling down the low brushwood under his feet, and tearing away all the minor branches that obstruct his impetuous progress.

It cannot however be denied, that there is a servile and a crouching spirit in the Bar towards the Bench, inconsistent with the equality on which all gentlemen are placed, and with the liberal nature of their early education and attainments. It may perhaps be conceded, that a small portion of this subserviency may arise among the younger Barristers, from timidity or misapprehension, without attributing it to a baser motive; but in causes of importance, more especially where political questions are involved, where the reputation or the liberty of an individual is concerned, it is impossible to trust to them; they will not speak out with decision and fearlessness, for the consequences of doing so stare them full in the face; they therefore shrink from the performance of their duty; and rather abandon a man to a dungeon, than abandon their own hopes of success in their profession.* None of them seem to think that any thing can be got by a straight-backed though a respectful and decorous demeanour; and it cannot but excite a melancholy feeling, when we see so many young men every term flocking from our universities to our courts, to embrace a profession that requires such a perversion and prostration of intellect,—such a deadness to the most generous impulses of our nature, and such a desertion of all dignity and independence of spirit. Not that the Bench should not be treated with all becom-

---

* This remark is general: what exceptions may be made to it, and how far they will apply, we shall have an opportunity of stating, when we speak of individuals who, on particular occasions, have shewn more or less fortitude.

ing deference, but there is a deference due to ourselves and to the cause of truth and justice. When HONE, in the course of his late trials, asserted that there was not a single Counsel who would venture to support his own conscientious conviction against the opinion of a presiding Judge,—I will venture to say that there was not a single Barrister present, whose hollow bosom did not echo the sentence, and silently admit its truth!

How this state of things must make us long to see some gifted and high-hearted spirit rise from among the submissive crowd of wigs and gowns, to vindicate his profession, and prove that a great respect and veneration for the Judges of the land is consistent with a greater respect and veneration for his own independence of mind, and for the sacred principles of truth and impartiality!

MR. SCARLETT.

Omnibus enim rebus is, qui princeps in agendo est, ornatissimus et paratissimus esse debet.——Cic. in Q. Cæcilium.

ᴀɴ excellent writer has said, that "eloquence is the common child of freedom and knowledge;"* and the remark is verified, if verification were needed, by the present state of the English Bar, as I endeavoured to shew in the preceding introductory article, where, among other causes of the decline of oratory in our courts of justice, two are principally rested upon—the absence of nearly all independence of mind, and the confinement of knowledge almost to the mechanism and drudgery of the profession. In a soil so cold and shallow, eloquence can never flourish; it can never strike wide and deep the spreading roots

* Wynne's Eunomus.

through which it must draw its nourishment ; or if by any accident a seed should fall upon better ground, it can never attain luxuriance or perfection, if the blossoms and burgeons are so unmercifully cropped and clipped by the hand of self-sufficient authority.   If, for the sake of impartiality, it be admitted that efforts to break through the trammels are sometimes repressed by Lord Ellenborough, because he revolts at any attempt to impose upon the good sense of a jury, it must also be allowed, that it is at least very question-able whether such interference be a part of the province and duties of a judge ; whether one man has a right to assume that he sees more clearly than twelve others, whose under-standings he is to take under his protection ? But setting aside that point, it ought at least to be recollected, that though one individual may be gifted with extraordinary penetration, it does not follow, that his eleven brethren of the Bench possess the same faculty and in the same degree : indeed the contrary in most instances must be the fact; and supposing that the ends of justice are not often defeated by Lord Ellenborough's precipitation, by other judges she may be made a cruel instrument of oppression, because they may think fit to pursue a system of servile and contemptible imitation.

Yet the submissiveness, the crouching acquiescence, the want of independence of mind, so generally deplored, and which has led nearly to the total disuse of Advocates in political and party prosecutions, is not confined merely to the Court of King's Bench, where the Lord Chief Justice presides—the system of imitation extends to the Counsel as well as to the Court; and if the deference be not in all the Courts quite so humiliating, it only arises from the circumstance, that there, indictments for libels upon the government or officers of state are not heard. If however the *venue*, as it is called, be laid in the country, and not subsequently changed, the case is tried at the assizes before the judge who may happen to go that circuit; besides, any barrister in any of the courts may be heard in the King's Bench, if he will venture to take a brief on a party question, or if a defendent will venture to trust him with one; so that, in truth, it comes to pretty nearly the same thing. Throughout the whole of this part of the profession, with a few honorable exceptions (of which Mr. SCARLETT is undoubtedy one) there prevails the same sort of contempt for every species of attainment that is not subservient to the miserable technicalities that incumber their capacities. Some have never learnt any thing else; but others, and not a few, reject all their early acquirements and glory in the absurd intricacies of pleas, counterpleas, demurrers, rejoinders, rebutters, surrebutters, and all that heap of trash, which makes counsel rich and clients poor:—such are doubly despicable; the rest are mere low-souled blockheads—

> For sure a fool I do him firmly hold
> That loves his fetters though they be of gold.
>   *Sp. F. Q.* B. 3, C. 9.

That Mr. SCARLETT belongs to either of these classes no one will imagine for a moment, who has heard or seen any thing of the proceedings of our Courts within the last five or six years; yet there is not a man at the bar who has a stronger relish for the niceties and subtleties of his pursuit : his admiration seems even sometimes to extend to its complicated and absurd formalities ; but this is a mistake : he feels, I am convinced, as supreme a contempt for them as any generous free-spirited student, when first he sets himself to the hateful task of narrowing and subduing his intellect to the comprehension and application of them. He is a man of great ingenuity and acuteness,—capable of drawing the most subtle and delicate distinctions ; and while he despises the mere forms, invented like all other quackery to puzzle the ignorant, he enjoys the curious niceties and refinements to which they not unfrequently lead ; he delights in making them as clear to others as to himself, and his countenance, generally good-humoured, and always intelligent, lights up with peculiar brightness while illustrating a point of this kind. To use a phrase of Sir Thomas Brown, in his *Religio Medici,* he seems to take pleasure, in the first instance, in " posing the understanding," in losing it in the labyrinths of the law, and then in producing his clue, and shewing how simple the

whole matter was when properly viewed. In
this particular he stands almost alone; many
others perhaps can rival him in the faculty
of analysis or simplification, and the power
of confounding what is intelligible is a very
vulgar attainment among lawyers; but none
seem to possess the double quality of first involving a question and then explaining the
difficulty, as it were, by that very involution.
Until this is understood, Mr. SCARLETT would
appear a sort of contradiction of what is above
advanced; for he is a lover of learning and
of learned men, an admirer of art and its pro-
fessors—a man of liberal thoughts and liberal
acquirements, and yet, to cursory observers,
a lover of many of the technicalities of special
pleading.*

This extreme ingenuity and subtlety were
in some respects of more use to him before he

---

* It may be necessary to remark, that the word *pleading* is applied popularly in a very different sense to that
in which it is used by lawyers; with the latter, it means
merely the preparation of laborious formalities; and has
no reference to speeches either to the jury or to the
court. This perversion of the term of itself seems to
shew the perversion of the practice.

obtained a silk gown than at present: he has now deservedly become the leading Counsel of the court in which he practises—the King's Bench; and the greater part of his emoluments arise out of what is termed *Nisi prius* business, or the trial of actions before a jury. Arguments upon points of pleading, upon dry technicalities, as well indeed as upon more general questions of law, are chiefly confided to the juniors, who have more time to study the case, and to hunt up the authorities; for this reason, during term the seniors have apparently but little to do*—I mean, contrasted with the ostensibility and bustle of their engagements in the sittings: they are seldom employed but on matters immediately arising out of the suits they have conducted at *Nisi prius;* so that some of the peculiar gifts of Mr. SCARLETT are now very much thrown away. Indeed, at first, after he took his seat

* Perhaps this remark applies less to Mr. SCARLETT than to any other king's counsel, for his reputation is such, that he is often employed to argue matters of mere law, especially in that involved branch relating to settlements: yet he has hardly time to read his briefs, and frequently argues difficult questions *at sight,* much to the satisfaction of his clients.

within the bar, they were sometimes positively disadvantageous to him, for he not unfrequently refined beyond the comprehension
of the jury, who have been afraid, where the
main facts were with him, to give a verdict in
his favor, lest they should in a manner have
been cheated into it by the advocate.   Of
late, however, he has in a great degree overcome this propensity; yet it still remains a
drawback upon the praise which, in most
respects, he eminently deserves.

Although I have seen nothing of Mr. SCAR-
LETT but in public, he may be safely pro-
nounced to be a very accomplished, and
what usually follows, a most unaffected, unpretending man: he never quotes Greek to
a jury, (as was done by a late learned and
laughed-at lord,) though he has been heard to
repeat a few words to the Court: he sometimes, in his addresses, employs a line or two
from the Latin writers, but always rather as
if the sentence had involuntary escaped his
lips, than as if it had been studiously sought
for, and laboriously applied. False quan-
tities (a fault not avoided by all at the bar

who adventure upon learned citations) are never heard from him; and there is something peculiarly fascinating about his voice and pronunciation. He seems also to be sufficiently acquainted with modern languages, though he does not ostentatiously thrust them forward, in imitation of a paltry smatterer of the last generation of king's counsel, who, in the effort to shew his learning, invariably betrayed his ignorance.—Mr. SCARLETT's references to matters of history, or to general literature, are sparing; but they would probably be more common, did not the extent of his practice almost preclude him in ordinary cases from making long speeches. Though he is a very accomplished man, he is far from being a perfect orator: his voice is musical, and his action not offensive, though in too small a compass; but, with regard to language, he appears to have a contempt for every thing like pomp of diction; he forms his periods upon no model, shunning whatever may look like art and construction. He will usually prefer a short word to a long one, even though the latter would sometimes better suit his purpose, and add greatly to the force and fulness of the sentence; as if he were determined that he would not fall under the ordinary reproach—

—————————This lawyer hath swallowed
Some apothecaries bills or proclamations ;
And now the hard and indigestible words
Come up like stones we use to give our hawks.
Webster's Vittoria Corombona, A. 3.

His mode of speaking is therefore most unambitious; and even when he becomes energetic or empassioned, he rarely reaches eloquence—the sustained and heightened style—the *aureum flumen orationis*—is not his; and if he begins a sentence well, he seldom arrives at the conclusion on the same level. He is one of the very rare instances of men, who have extorted rank and secured emolument by little else than the mere force of talent; yet a few years ago, the defect just noticed was much more conspicuous in him than at present; his delivery was formerly even deficient in fluency; his words dropped out, two, three, or four at a time, leaving painful intervals, that much interfered with the impressiveness of his delivery : at that period, also, he more frequently destroyed the force of the beginning of his sentences, by the awkward manner in which he concluded them; the first of these defects he has however now entirely conquered, and the last is neither so common nor so obvious.

The business of a leading council at *Nisi prius* chiefly consists of opening speeches, in which the facts are detailed, of the examination of witnesses, and of replies to the case made out on the other side. It is in the last that Mr. SCARLETT is principally eminent, since he has overcome, in a great measure, his refining inclination; his openings are not remarkable for any thing but distinctness, and an endeavour, carried too far, to answer the supposed case of his adversary, instead of relying upon and enforcing his own: the effect *is, that* he now and then raises ill-founded suspicions in the minds of the jurymen, that he has not much confidence on what his own witnesses will establish. His examinations and cross examinations are not deficient in art or shrewdness, but they are not to be compared with those of Sir William Garrow or Lord Erskine: they want much of the intuition of the former, and of the humourous

D

wheedling of the latter, by which he not unfrequently convinced an adverse witness, that
he was his friend and not his enemy. Mr
SCARLETT however has strength without un-
gentlemanliness, and he generally is successfu
in extracting the truth. His ruddy, smiling
contented countenance, often deceives a wit
ness into a belief, that whether his answer b
no or yes, is a matter of perfect indifference
His replies are however his great *forte*—th
excellence of some of them has perhaps neve
been exceeded. If the issue depend upon th
balance of testimony, upon contradictory wit
nesses, there is no man, and perhaps neve
was a man, who had a happier facility o
displaying the weak parts of his opponent'
case and the strong parts of his own. If i
depend upon a deduction of inferences, upor
the combination of many minute circumstances, upon reconciling apparently discordant evidence, he is sure to obtain attention ir
the commencement, and to rivet it to the conclusion. He makes few or no notes of what he
intends to say, but arranges all the points ir
his memory; and when he rises, his face ex-
presses the certainty of a verdict in his favour.

He is never tedious, and his remarks upon
trifles never seem frivolous or unnecessary
he never exhausts his hearers, and always his
subject.

Before I conclude, let me do this gentleman
the justice to observe, that he is to a considerable extent one of the exceptions to that
crouching servility of the bar I referred to in
my last article; he is obviously a gentleman
in his feelings, and of course a gentleman in
his conduct; but I have seen him (and I
acknowledge it with pleasure) make a firm
though respectful resistance to what he considered the unjust dictation of the Bench; it
is fit however to add, that no political question was involved in the result.

Since I wrote the preceding article Mr.
SCARLETT has taken his seat in the House of
Commons, and has started as a parliamentary
speaker: the occasions on which he has delivered his opinions have not been numerous,
but sufficiently so to shew that though he will
never be an orator, he is a good debater, and

would be a better, did not his professiona
avocations demand so much of his time.   Th
opposition look upon him as an able sup
porter, and so he undoubtedly is, at a tim
when, with two or three exceptions, there i
such a lack of talent, and almost a total ab
sence of eloquence on that, and indeed on th
other, side of the House.   The sort of ski
Mr. SCARLETT, exhibits in court accompa
nies him into parliament.

I may take this opportunity of mentionin
that several persons whose judgment I respec
are of opinion, that I have given in some pa
ticulars too high a character of Mr. SCAF
LETT, especially where I say that he is "ur
affected and unpretending."—I do not thin
so; and as I speak my own sentiments, an
not those of others, I have made no alteratio
Perhaps he has in a slight degree the defec
of superciliousness; I am not aware, howevei
that this has increased with his honours, an
perhaps more originates in an unwillingnes
to be supposed to court the favour of the in
feriors of his profession than from a natura
haughtiness of disposition.

MR. MARRYAT.

Long dash ——————— The law to him
Is like a foul black cobweb to a spider;
He makes it his dwelling, and a prison
To entangle those that feed him.

Webster's Duchess of Malfy, A. 1.

THOSE who think with Bishop Hall, "woe
to the weal where many lawyers thrive,"
would augur very ill of the state of this
country from the fact, that there is, perhaps,
no profession at present so much over-stocked
in all its departments as the law; shoals of
attornies are sworn in daily every succeeding
term, and the number of barristers called by
the various societies is very nearly, if not
quite in proportion. That part of the area of
our Courts, especially of the King's Bench,
devoted to the accommodation of the latter,

is more than twice as large as the space appropriated to solicitors, suitors, and the public; yet in term-time it is crowded to excess, and whether the business of the day be important or trifling makes little or no difference to those who fill it : the great majority do not attend to profit by displays of genius, learning, or ingenuity, in an eloquent speech or a logical argument, but to collect and register insignificant points of practice or pleading—whether such and such a rule is made absolute in the first instance, or whether such and such facts warrant an action of *assumpsit* or trespass.

> They pick up *law* as pidgeons pick up peas,
> To deal it forth again—as Heaven doth please.

An appeal as to the correctness of what I have advanced, might safely be made to the margin-crammed note-books, which these indefatigable gentlemen always carry about them. Some listless supporters of wigs and gowns, it is true, are only lawyers in externals —mere idlers and loungers, who stroll down to Westminster-Hall, because they have nothing to do any where else—to loll upon

the benches, gossip, and crack a few bad
jokes ; but their number is small compared
with those, who having spent years in plea
ders' offices, learning little else but to forge
the knowledge they had previously acquired
visit our Courts to witness the application o
all the useless and cumbrous forms with which
the law is now overloaded. These men
when first they are called, take their seat
upon the back-row most distant from the
court, content to be numbered and not named
when the bar is gone through*. Now and
then they are favoured by some friendly
attorney with a motion of course, or perhaps
one of them obtains a junior brief on the
circuit, which makes him fortunately known
to a particular judge: that judge condescend
to call upon him by name in the following
term, and it is met by a smile of peculiar
gratitude, and a bow of unusual servility
Some legal friend, who stood in our young
barrister's way, then fortunately dies, and he

* " To go through the Bar" is a sort of law idiom, and
signifies calling upon the counsel according to seniorit
when they have any motions to make.

immediately steps into his business—he "obtains the ear of the Court," by following the example of his predecessors,

——————————— Da i piu sublimi
Ad ubbidire imparino i piu bassi,—

Tasso. Ger. Lib.

and business follows of course. He now advances with confidence to the front rows, and in due time is honoured with a silk gown, and with the title of "one of his Majesty's Counsel learned in the law."

Such, generally speaking, is the progress of a barrister before he arrives at the very highest honours of the profession, though it is not to be denied that real learning and true talent will to a certain degree force their own way, and extort reluctant distinction. Indeed an instance of it to a certain extent I gave in the preceding article, and Mr. MARRYAT (who for that reason principally is now selected) in a very limited degree deserves the same praise; for though far inferior to Mr. Scarlett, he has worked his way upwards often under the frowns of the bench. In no other particular however can any comparison for a moment be made.

The fact, however, of the advance of Mr. MARRYAT, though slow (for he was called to the bar when very young), proves that he must have some merit; but the principal difficulty is to discover in what it consists. His great qualification certainly is a know-ledge of the heavy business of his profession— an acquaintance with all the elaborate intri-cacies that belong to it; but it is impossible to contend that he is not lamentably wanting in all kinds of general information, and igno-rant even of the higher branches of his own pursuit. When therefore I say that he is a man of more learning than talent, it is not placing the latter very high, because the former is so limited in its range; and when I add, that he is a lawyer, I do not mean even that he is a man of deep research in his profession—who has studied the sources and foundations of law, its first principles, and their subsequent extension and appli-cation. The rise and progress of the law,

as a science, probably never entered into
his contemplation; he has been contented to
take things as he found them, and perhaps
the greatest praise he deserves is that he has
made himself pretty thoroughly intimate with
them. Why they are as they are, and why
they are not as they ought to be, he would
deem a most useless, because unprofitable,
inquiry. Surely it would be expected of a
King's counsel learned in the law, that he
should at least be instructed in the events of
our national history, yet even some of these
and their consequences and bearings he is
obviously in the dark about, and no one
will be inclined to presume any thing in
favour of an individual who makes it his
boast that since he left school he has never
read any but a law book. I do not wish to
be understood that he is upon a level with an
Irish barrister, who referring to two great
events, the obtaining Magna Charta, and
the Bill of Rights, confounded the sove-
reigns from whom they were exacted; nor
with the celebrated English barrister, who
having occasion to quote a statute, and being

required to mention the period at which i
passed, very gravely replied, that it was ir
the reign of one of the Henrys, or one of the
Edwards, but he could not exactly tel
which: ordinary conversation, and the in
dorsements upon his Ruffhead, supposing h
never opened it, would afford sufficien
instruction to avoid such exposures. Ther
is no doubt, however, that he is what woul
be considered in well-educated society—tha
society for which his rank qualifies him—a
ignorant man. To the court nor to the jur
does he ever address a remark or make ar
allusion which would lead an auditor to
suppose that he had acquired a particle o
any but legal knowledge since he was free
from scholastic castigations ; on the contrar
so constantly is every opportunity permitte
to escape, that it would almost be conclude
that he had totally forgotten what he mus
formerly have learnt. I heard Mr. Scarle
once introduce a Latin quotation by observing
that there was something in the air of court
of law that drove all matters of taste out c
the head, and he seemed feelingly to lamen

the loss. Mr. MARRYAT could not participate either in the regret or its occasion ; at the same time I do not go so far as to believe all the current stories against him ; on the contrary, the assertion that he once applied for two *mandami* is most likely a libel upon his latinity.

About modern languages, so often useful to others, he seems to know nothing, and to care less : in the true spirit of John Bull, he apparently despises all foreigners but those who happen to be his clients.

Though he is not remarkable for acuteness, he is not deficient in quickness ; and if it be asked how he obtained so large a share of business, the answer is, that he is principally indebted for it, not to his talents, but to his most laborious and plodding industry : he has gradually and slowly worked his way, and has gained the character among the attornies of being a very solid man : indeed a better authority cannot be consulted upon the heavy drudgery of the profession.   His opinions may be generally relied upon ; and while there are few counsel who have more cases to answer, none takes more pains with, or bestows more time upon them. His lega' arguments are overburdened with authorities, but without arrangement, and his knowledge seems disposed in his head, pretty much in the same order as furniture in an upholsterer's shop.

He is one of the most clumsy, negligen' speakers that ever opened his lips: it has often been remarked of the present Lord Chie: Justice, that he never ends a sentence, and Mr. MARRYAT, it may be added, nevei begins one : he involves his speech in innu merable parentheses, and connects the mos' discordant parts by his favourite words, *and, but*, and *so ;* running on at a hand-gallop dashing through thick and thin, floundering here and stumbling there, and bespattering al who come in his way. Indeed he possesse: very few qualifications for a *nisi prius* advo cate, and in this respect he has been out o his element ever since he exchanged hi:

E

bombazeen for silk. Formerly, upon commercial questions, bankruptcies, and matters
relating to shipping and navigation, he was
at least tolerable ; but it is now quite laugh-
able to hear him attempt to open a case that
requires any thing like choice of language or
oratorical display : an appeal to the feelings
of a jury, or a speech in mitigation of da-
mages from him, rather serves to shew the
student what he ought to shun, than what he
ought to say.   He has always the merit of
being zealous, but it often occasions an exag-
geration of his faults.   A French satirist
asserts that " anger sometimes produces the
same effect as inspiration,"* but though it is
not true of poetry, it is now and then verified
in public speaking, and at such a time I
have heard Mr. MARRYAT forcible and affec-
tive ; but if the stream be strong it is always
muddy ; when energetic he is never select in
his epithets ; and, as Lord Ellenborough once
said of a witness, " really such men should

---

* Et sans aller rêver dans le double vallon
   La colère suffit, et vaut un Apollon.
                              Boileau, Sat. I.

not venture upon metaphor." Mr. MAR-
RYAT's best effort of this kind is a speech to
evidence; but still a want of arrangemen
very much destroys the effect of his obser
vations : his formal objections, or what is
called picking a hole in a declaration, are
not unfrequently successful.

The action employed by him is the most
inappropriate that could be used : while his
head and full round shining face are in vigorous motion, shaking from side to side in the
vehemence of vociferation, his arms are
buckled close to his sides, and his fingers
are actively employed in buttoning and
unbuttoning his coat, or in twiddling the
strings of his gown. As may be guessed,
his wig is often thrown awry by the violence
of the action of his head ; and the adjusting
of it (when he thinks it necessary, which is
not always the case) forms an agreeable
diversity. For the same reason, one is unwilling to object to the not very graceful
mode in which he puts both hands behind
him, and tucks up his robe, so as to form an

artificial projection in the rear to balance the natural protuberance in the front. Leaning both hands upon the table, and swaying backwards and forwards, is the highest perfection he has in this respect yet reached, or probably will ever attain.

From what has been observed, it will not be thought very high praise to say, that at *nisi prius* Mr. MARRYAT's chief excellence consists in the mode in which he examines or cross-examines a witness: nothing ruffles him; nothing puts him out of his straightforward course: a retort never disturbs him. We are told that the late Mr. Bearcroft was disconcerted by an old woman in a brewery cause, who called him Mr. *Beercraft*; but the gentleman of whom we are now speaking can put up with the most insolent replies with the utmost composure: he always affects not to hear what makes against his side of the question, and follows up the answer so quickly with another interrogatory, that he sometimes succeeds in suppressing it. This indeed is the only piece of artifice or address

he uses; and if the Counsel on the other side
interposes, or even if the Judge interferes,
Mr. MARRYAT carries it off with a great
appearance of innocent unconsciousness. He
does not pretend to much ingenuity in framing
his questions, or in planning the course of an
examination; this is a refinement of art he
never will attain. He is obstinately persevering in his inquiries, and a witness never
gains his point by not giving an answer as
direct as the question; for Mr. MARRYAT
is so patient, that he will repeat the same
words over and over again twenty times until
his object is accomplished.

There is, however, one great perfection
about him, not at all connected with his
talents, that more than any other secures him
the good opinion of the suitors, though not
the good will of the Court. The summary
manner in which causes are referred at *nisi
prius*, frequently in direct opposition to the
declared wishes, and probably interests, of the
parties, because it may happen to suit the
views or convenience of the presiding Judge,

has often been reprobated, not merely by sufferers. The Counsel who have pocketed all their fees are well contented to be spared the trouble of earning them, while the plaintiff and defendant are not uncommonly put to 20*l*., 50*l*., or even 100*l*. additional charges as the costs of the reference. ' This injurious practice has lately been censured from the highest authority ; for the Lord Chancellor declared, in the case of Willan *v.* Willan, in the Autumn of 1818, that, if he were at the bar, he would compel a Judge to try a cause, on which he thought the opinion of a Jury ought to be taken. Had he been only a Counsel, his language would most likely have been different, for ordinarily the profound deference shewn to the slightest hint from the Bench produces at most a very gentle opposition, or perhaps none at all. In this respect Mr. MARRYAT, more than any other man in his situation, deserves approbation : he has been known to struggle to the end of a trial with the most zealous perseverance, after repeated recommendations by the Judge to refer the matter in difference ; and though this obstinacy (as it was called) would, perhaps, in most cases, be impolitic for his client, as causes are now conducted, yet in this instance he obtained and merited a verdict.

Of wit or humour Mr. MARRYAT has not a particle: he probably never made nor relished a joke in his life; but he is not deficient in good sense and its companion—discretion. His greatest excellence is zeal, and his greatest defect ignorance.

MR. SERGEANT BEST.

Quick wits be commonly apt to take, unapt to keep; more quick to enter speedily, than able to pierce far; even like oversharp tools whose edges be very soon turned.——Roger Ascham's Schoolmaster.

WHEN we reflect upon the many qualifications necessary for a perfect advocate, according to the mode in which law is now administered in this country;—when we remember that he must possess much more than the great pattern of eloquence required in an orator;—that he ought to be gifted not only with extraordinary powers of language—with great learning, general and particular, but also with discretion and a peculiar quickness, acumen, and cunning, apparently inconsistent with his higher and nobler faculties,

it makes us despair of ever beholding at ou
bar an individual so endowed. Experienc
too shews, that such despair is not ill-founded
for most of the qualifications above enume
rated are rare even in their separate excellence
and few have ever figured in the professioi
who have enjoyed more than two or three ii
combination. To go no further back than th
memory of some of our younger legal aspirant
—Mingay was shrewd and forcible, but vaii
and ignorant ; Erskine was eloquent anc
energetic, but wanted much legal knowledg
and a little legal cunning; Garrow hac
quickness and cunning beyond any of hi
rivals, but was deficient in the lowest element
of learning ; and Gibbs, with scholarship
a knowledge of his profession, both in it
magnitude and in its minuteness, had scarcelj
a spark of eloquence, and was outwitted bj
men of half his talents and one tenth-part o
his attainments. But as there are in the law sc
many different departments, room is found
for men of all kinds—the dullest can obtaii
employment, and the brightest, if he will ai
first condescend to a few of the tricks ol

trade, and if he have sufficient firmness, may make occasions for the display of his powers.

The subject of the present criticism is taken from the Court of Common Pleas, with the proceedings of which the public at large is comparatively but little acquainted. The smallness of all our Courts renders it impossible that many visitors should be admitted ; and, generally speaking, an opinion is formed of the merits of Advocates from the reports in the newspapers of trials in which they have been concerned : but it is somewhat singular, that while every day a long detail is given of the business of the King's Bench, little or no notice is taken of the Common Pleas. It has surprised many persons, that while in the former the cause-paper is over-loaded, so that one Judge is almost incompetent to superintend the decisions, in the latter they are comparatively few, though frequently important. Some have attributed this disparity to a want of confidence in the Judges; but surely this is paying an ill-compliment to the understanding of the juries. Supposing however this conjecture to a certain extent correct, I feel convinced, that did our public journals pay more attention to the business of the Common Pleas, the actions there tried would very soon be multiplied: plaintiffs, who do not generally object to publicity, though defendants may shun it, are unwilling to institute a proceeding in a place where it will probably never be heard of beyond the walls; and they are besides probably little acquainted with the qualifications of the various counsel, whose practice in London is chiefly confined to that Court. Yet it is an almost undisputed fact, by those whose business it is to attend to the proceedings in Westminster-Hall, that the advocates in the Common Pleas, as a body, are superior to those of the King's Bench.

In two important particulars the former have a decided advantage over their rivals; the one results from the smaller number of actions they have to try, and the longer time that may consequently be devoted to them;

so that a serjeant has more favourable opportunities of employing his oratorical talents; the
other is, that the judges in the Common Pleas
do not exercise quite the same controul over
the sergeants. Perhaps this may result partly
from the equality of *brotherhood*, which they
recognize whenever they make a remark; but
it principally arises from other circumstances:
—true it is, that one or two of the judges
have endeavoured to assert and maintain an
authority equal to that of the Lord Chief
Justice of the King's Bench; but the only
one of them who has any pretensions to such
a sway is Sir V. Gibbs, who very seldom presides.* Mr. Justice Dallas is too much of
a gentleman to engage in the contest; Mr.
Justice Burrough is too recently elevated to
risk it, and Mr. Justice Park—but he is too
properly appreciated to need the assignment
of any reason why his influence is not greater
either with attornies or counsel, whenever he
happens to be upon the bench at *nisi prius*.

* He has now retired, and has been succeeded as Chief
Justice of the Common Pleas by Sir Robert Dallas, who
is a pattern of deportment in his high station.

F

But it is time to speak of Mr. Sergeant BEST, who is one of the principal ornaments of this Court, and who enjoys the greatest share of business; I do not hesitate to say, that his qualifications as an advocate before a jury (for I here confine myself to that) are probably more eminent than those of any other man now practising in Westminster-hall. In particular points probably several individuals could be named who are his equals, if not his superiors—one in legal knowledge, another in perspicuity, a third in subtlety,

Qui juris nodos, et legum ænigmata solvat ;—

but most of these have little or nothing else to recommend them, and either of those qualities alone, or even one or two of them united in the same person, are insufficient. Mr. Sergeant BEST however possesses perspicuity and acuteness, if it do not amount to subtlety, in a very striking degree, and they are combined with several other important requisites noticed in the commencement. In mere legal knowledge, the dry business of the profession,

he is unquestionably somewhat defective, and
to legal learning, if I may use the distinction,
he makes no pretension. Let me add however, that of the former he is not by any means
ignorant; for constant practice, even without
study, must unavoidably have communicated
to him some information relative to the forms
and machinery of the law; he has not, like
many legal pedants, devoted his whole reading to them; he has left them to mechanical
heads competent to nothing else; he has however imperceptibly become familiar with the
more useful parts even of this branch; a man
like him need not sit down as an ordinary
plodder in pleas and demurrers, to hammer
things through the substance of his skull; he
obtains in such matters what some call an
instinctive knowledge, because they are unable to trace how it is acquired.

His general information regarding literature, the arts, and matters of taste, is principally of the same kind, for he does not appear to have been very regularly educated
he has however mixed with the world, (o

which indeed a court of justice may be considered in some sort an epitome,) and, aware probably of his own deficiencies, he seems to have taken pains to supply them; and his knowledge, at least of the superficies of things, is such, and his prudence and ingenuity in turning all he gains to the best account so great, that he seldom or never betrays his ignorance.   Yet there are not a few lawyers, who, because he happens not to have trodden in the laborious, tangled, and lower walks of the profession, affect to look upon him as a pretender: when he is successfully addressing a jury, they will sometimes be heard to mutter with a sneer, that he is vapid or frivolous, by which is to be understood only that they do not possess the eloquence he is displaying, and which they have not generosity enough to acknowledge.   At the same time, I am quite ready to allow all that can be fairly said against the solidity of his attainments; all I contend for is, the superiority of his natural powers, improved and almost perfected by habit.   Undoubtedly he is one of those " quick wits, apt to take but unapt to keep;

more quick to enter speedily than to pierce far;" but then I answer that this aptness to take, and this faculty of entering speedily into a subject, is exactly what is most wanted in a *nisi prius* counsel ; heavy learning may sometimes, but will not often, be useful, and slowness of perception and comprehension can never be of the slightest advantage to any man in any situation.

From what has been said, it will be gathered, that I think highly of the oratorical powers of Mr. Sergeant BEST. I am inclined to believe, that few men of late years, (perhaps none since the time of Erskine,) have at times gained more influence not only over the feelings but sometimes even over the understandings of a jury. His general stile of speaking is extremely energetic and forcible —his heart always seems to be in what he is uttering, and in such a case it seldom happens that he does not carry the hearts of his hearers along with him : yet notwithstanding his great practice, he is not always fluent ; he has been known even to make a dead stand,

and has not very unfrequently a hesitation,
which proceeds not from a want of words,
but from a superabundance of thoughts ; his
mind is so full of what he ought to say, that
the ordinary channel seems choked, and it
runs over and interrupts the regular stream
of his utterance.   In one view this is a draw-
back upon his impressiveness ; but as it is
said that "some mens' excellences serve them
but as enemies," so his defects sometimes serve
him as friends, for this very hesitation begets
a strong interest in his favor.   Mr. Justice
Dallas, who when at the bar was one of its
most elegant and accomplished orators, never
began a speech without much of this apparent difficulty of enunciation ;   in him it was
originally the effect of art, but with Mr. Sergeant BEST it is the effect of nature, and the
consequence of zealous impetuosity.   His
whole style is unstudied and free from any
kind of affectation ; when he says any thing
well, it is always without effort ; and though
he very rarely attempts a florid ornamental
or even a declamatory manner, he seldom
renders it painful by failure, or offensive by

overstrained exertion. He has not much fancy or imagination, (as the terms are indifferently used,) and does not affect to speak as if he had.

His action is like his speaking, easy without carelessness, and varied without pretence : perhaps he uses his right hand too much—or I should say, his left hand too little : for he has such an impressive and imposing way of stretching forth his right hand, when he is pathetically endeavouring to work upon the minds of the jury, that his hearers would much regret to see it restrained. He has besides the advantage of a sharp piercing eye, and an animated countenance capable of great variety of expression. It used to be said of Sir W. Garrow, that he was an actor as well as an advocate—that when silent, he ceased not to address the jury by the change of his features ; to a certain degree, this power is enjoyed and employed by Mr. Sergeant BEST : it is much the same as the bye-play upon the stage, and some counsel, whose leaden visages can express little else

but their dullness, call it unfair and u
manly. They forget or never knew
advocate is nothing but an actor, w
the Italian *improvisatoræ* players, in
dialogue of his own part, the plot bei
plied him; and they might just as
ably object to his being eloquent, becau
cannot put three sentences together, a
availing himself of this or any of th
faculties God has bestowed upon him.

In another respect, also, he makes a
approach to the excellence of Sir W. G
than any other man at the bar, no
cepting Mr. Scarlett,—I mean the m
which he worms out the truth and ex
the guilt of a profligate witness :—Mr
geant BEST is always ready with expe
which he can vary indefinitely; he pro
by slow and wily degrees—winds roun
purpose—detects first one falsehood,
another, until the witness is confounde
his complicated perjuries, and is at last
pelled to free himself by avowing the t
Sir W. Garrow saw through a desig

scoundrel at a glance,—the vicious to him were, as Sterne supposes men in the planet Mercury,—absolutely vitrified: he beheld the darkest and deepest workings of the heart by a perfect intuition; and in this faculty Mr. Sergeant BEST is far his inferior, for it is quite independent of acuteness or cunning; he dares not, like Sir W. Garrow, attack a smooth hypocrite point-blank, exposing his falsehood, and certain of success, while by-standers, not in the secret, are astonished at his hardihood. This constitutes the chief difference between these two individuals, for in point of shrewdness and ingenuity in putting a question, they may be considered nearly upon a level: but Mr. Sergeant BEST is obliged to be more wary, to take more care that he stands upon solid ground, lest by im-puting untruth to a witness, he make the jury revolt at his unjust severity.

There is one peculiarity about this gentle-man that deserves remark:—

Nulla ferè causa est, in quâ non fæmina litem
Moverit,—

says the satirist, and it is probably as true of London as of Rome : at least, if causes here do not so frequently owe their origin to women, it very seldom happens, unless it be merely a commercial matter, that a woman has not something to do with them, either as a promoter, a party, or a witness. Now Mr. Sergeant BEST, though not young, and though much tormented by the gout, is a man of considerable gallantry, in the ordinary sense of the word : of course, this has reference only to what passes in court, where he always seems to treat the softer sex with peculiar lenity ; if it fall to his lot to examine a pretty girl, on whatever side she is a witness, he can scarcely find in his heart to be the least uncivil to her. Let her evidence be what it may, he appears to look upon her as " a palace for the crowned truth to dwell in," and he cannot easily be brought to believe, that falsehood may have there taken up its abode. At least this is an error on the right side ; great consideration is undoubtedly due to a female in such an unwonted situation, and great delicacy in not unnecessarily insulting

her by imputations upon her veracity can
hardly be imputed as a fault to any man
It much too frequently happens, that witnesses of this sex are treated with needles
rudeness, if not with wanton coarseness.

This then is the general summary of the
merits and defects of Mr. Sergeant BEST : he
is superficial, both in legal and in general
knowledge; but his talents and his prudence
enable him to bring his small stock to the
best market : he is eloquent in speech, and
impressive in action ; he is acute, ready, and
ingenuous : let him be assisted by a junior
council, who can answer formal objections,
and success is very possible in a bad, but
almost certain in a good cause. With his
political conduct and opinions I have nothing
to do, and I am glad of it.

Mr. Sergeant BEST is now raised to the
office of a judge, and sits in the Court of
King's Bench. It follows of course that his

class of talents is there almost thrown away, while he probably has sufficient sensibility to regret the absence of more solid qualities and attainments.   Men of his stamp seem not born for such situations, and after admiring them at the bar, it cannot but excite a strong feeling of regret to see them thus laid upon a high shelf, out of the sphere in which they have long moved, and to which they belong. I never look at Mr. Baron Garrow, in the Court of Exchequer, without a *heu! quantum mutatus.*

THE ATTORNEY GENERAL.

These be they that use men's writings like brute
beasts, to make them draw which way they list.
T. Nash's Lenten Stuff, 1599.

OF all offices in the gift of the Crown that of
Attorney-general is perhaps least to be coveted;
for whether the Government be popular or
unpopular, the person filling that place can
scarcely avoid being the object of general
dislike: the rank is only fourth or fifth rate,
and the manner in which it has been attained
is always suspected, though sometimes un-
justly: he is pretty sure to be charged with
having ascended by the usual steps of political fawning and judicial servility, and after

all he is only to be considered as the servant of servants—the curse of the Israelites. Lord Bacon says, that men in high stations are thrice servants—of the King, of the State, and of the time—but the Attorney General is obliged to submit to a quadruple servitude; or at least he must endure the charge of submitting to it, though it may be less in fact than in appearance. But this, to a barrister who has been under a sort of submissive pupilage all his life, one may suppose to be the least part of the irksomeness of his situation, though the present Attorney-General, Sir SAMUEL SHEPHERD, seemed to feel very acutely upon the subject on one or two occasions.*

The most unpleasant consequence of all however appears to be, that the nation at

* Wooler, in the course of his his trials on two *ex-officio* informations for libels, asserted that the Attorney-General had been obliged to obey the orders of ministers, his *masters;* but Sir S. SHEPHERD interrupted him not only once or twice with the words—"Sir, I have no masters." If I recollect rightly, the same sort of thing happened when Hone was before the Court of King's Bench.

large must look upon the Attorney-General
as a sort of ministerial spy—an informer of
rather a higher rank than those who have
recently become notorious; whose business
it is to ferret out and prosecute all who, either
by their actions or writings, are endeavouring
to displace the personages to whom he is indebted for his situation, or who are attempting to promote any reform in the system
they support. Most of the ministry are engaged in great questions of foreign policy
(or, at all events, affect to be so) in establishing dynasties and settling transferrences of
territory and subjects, and they leave the
Attorney-General to bear the brunt at home;
his hand may be said to be against every
body, and every body's hand against him;
he must fight all their domestic battles, and
repel and punish all attacks whether political or personal; he must revenge all the little
party quarrels

Of those great men who clothe their private hate
In the fair colours of the public good;
And to effect their ends pretend the State,
As if the State by their affections stood.

S. Daniel's Philotas, A. 3.

Thus the responsibility of the Attorney-General is not only weighty but peculiar. A minister, if he fail in any undertaking, excites the national displeasure, but contrives to keep his place; he throws the blame upon his agents and underlings; or if he cannot do that, the public disapprobation is easily borne; it is too broad to press severely from any particular quarter, and " enough for virtue is her own applause!" Not so with the Attorney-General—if he fail in any prosecution, he incurs first the displeasure of his employers, (*Masters* I will not call them out of delicacy to the feelings of Sir SAMUEL SHEPHERD;) then the particular hostility of the individuals proceeded against; next he loses the confidence of the friends of ministers; and lastly he gains the contempt and ridicule of their enemies.

With such imminent hazards, it seems singular at first sight that any man can be induced to accept such a situation: the temptation is, that it often leads to the highest honors of the profession, not improbably to a peerage; but even then few but lawyers,

who all their lives, as it were, have run the
gauntlet of difficulties and dilemmas, with
the sole purpose of gaining money and gratifying ambition, could be found to undertake
its burdensome duties. It seems, however, of
late, as if the temptation had been less and
the hazards greater; for we have seen instances where Attornies-General have gained
nothing, or less than nothing, by all their
exertions in favour of their patrons : witness
the individual who was recently compelled
to forsake a business of scarcely less than
15,000l. a year, and to withdraw into what
has been called " an honourable retirement,'
as one of the puisne barons of the Exchequer.*

---

* The motto he has chosen on his *elevation* to the Bench
seems singularly inappropriate—*Concussus surgo :* it
is almost like a satire upon himself and his fallen fortunes ; perhaps a good-natured friend, when consulted
mistranslated the words to him.—*Providentiæ me com-
mitto* is the inscription under the arms of another learned
Judge, who has made himself notorious on the Western
Circuit : his friends recommend him to attend to his
pious motto and trust to heaven ; for assuredly he ough
not to trust to himself, if there be any truth in the
stories lately told of him.

Perhaps there never was a more unfortu-:unate Attorney-General than Sir SAMUEL SHEPHERD : he has proceeded against libel-lers personal and official—against parodists of the sacred ritual of the church—and against persons accused of the heinous crime of trea-son : his attempts have had great variety in their object and great uniformity in their result : I do not recollect that he has obtained a single conviction in London ; yet his failures have not arisen from want of zealous exertion on his part, nor from superiority of talent on the part of the defendants ; they frequently pleaded their own causes, and though one of these shop-orators (as they are vulgarly termed) was tolerable in point of fluency; he was execrable in point of style, and betrayed his ignorance and want of education in every sentence* True it is that the Attorney-Gene-

* I mean Mr. Wooler, of whom I know nothing, and wish to know nothing, beyond what I saw of him on his :rials ; his speeches have been much and undeservedly praised : for his fame he is chiefly indebted to the reporters of the newspapers, and for his liberty to the blunders of the jury. Mr. Hone is I believe a respectable bookseller, without pretensions, and in my judgment is not only a better informed man, but in most essentials a better speaker than Mr. Wooler.

ral succeeded in procuring the execution of some of the Derby rioters ; but this is almost the only instance in which he has prevailed in the country, and the last and most signal discomfiture was atchieved by a female antagonist in Cornwall.*

Yet notwithstanding these defects—notwithstanding the frequent occasions on which he has " made a scare-crow of the regal name," and himself in some sort " a fool for public use." Sir SAMUEL SHEPHERD is still respected by most of his friends in office, and perhaps there never was a man who had to fulfil the ungrateful duties of Attorney-General who had fewer enemies, both personal and political. But though his patrons may respect him, they feel no great warmth of attachment, for services rendered or expected, (the only bonds of men in office,) and shew no strong desire further to advance him

---

* Miss Tocker.—He did not conduct this prosecution in person, nor was it I believe by information *ex-officio* it was an indictment for a libel upon a ministerial deputy, the Vice-warden of the Stannary court.

His deafness is undoubtedly a considerable impediment, but he is probably soon destined for some other " honourable retirement," to make room for a new ambitionist, who may promise more and cannot well perform less ; for some aspiring apostate, who having been professionally educated how to take any side in the court, has been ministerially instructed how to take any side in the House.   For such a one it will most likely be found that Sir SAMUEL SHEPHERD will vacate his office : if he filled it without success, he obtained it without tergiversation.*   He has however been unfortunate, not merely because he could not procure verdicts against Wooler or Hone,

---

* It was long reported at the Bar, and believed, that Sir S. SHEPHERD was to be made accountant-general at the death of Mr. Smith, who, probably much to the dissatisfaction of ministers, continues hale and hearty, and eats his dinners in Middle Temple Hall with a good appetite. It now however appears (July, 1819) that he is to be created Chief Baron of the Exchequer in Scotland.——It is stated that his predecessor in this office had received several gentle hints that his services were no longer required, and it was a strange coincidence, that on the very day when Sir S. SHEPHERD was appointed, the late Chief Baron died.

but because he was compelled to bring thes
cases and others into Court : the information
were not filed by him, but by his predecesso
Sir W. Garrow; they were almost the la:
efforts of the Baron of the Exchequer to mer:
a continuance of the favour of his patrons
and of course at such a time, when threatene
with expulsion, he would be doubly anxiou
to give extraordinary proofs of his zea
towards them, and of his hostility toward
their enemies. Sir SAMUEL SHEPHERD foun
these and more in his office when he entere
it, and he could not turn them out withou
bringing them to trial, whether he considere
the respect due to his precursor, or the avowe
wishes of those who had just bestowed thei
smiles upon him. It is felt therefore by on
party, that the ill success is not entirely at
tributable to him, and by the other, that ha
he been Attorney-General at an earlier dat
the informations would probably not hav
been filed. The good-natured public re
collect too, that though he prosecuted an
advised the prosecution of those mischievou
but contemptible semi-ideots, Preston, Wat

son, and others, the plot was not of his brewing : it had been *doctored* in another quarter, and his aid was not required until it had probably been so worked up that he could not easily discover the substance on account of the froth* It is proper also to add, in this place, that very few *ex-officio* proceedings indeed have been instituted by Sir SAMUEL SHEPHERD since he was entrusted with this onerous discretion.

The foregoing remarks, not indeed purely political, have been made for the purpose of exemplifying the real character of the individual whose conduct and talents are the subject of the present article, and of shewing why he is in some degree an exception to the position with which I set out, that an Attorney General could scarcely avoid becoming an object of public dislike. If it be said that I am travelling out of my course in touching

---

* If I remember rightly, he confessed in Parliament, after the trials, that Ministers had not let him into the secret of the real character of the celebrated witness Mr. Castles.

upon political topics, which hitherto have been carefully avoided, my answer is short and plain—that the Attorney and Solicitor-General are to be contemplated not merely as Advocates, but as Government Advocates, and that their conduct in office cannot be separated from the view of their qualifications for the stations they occupy ; in forming an estimate of their talents and learning, the sphere in which they have been employed cannot possibly be disregarded. I will now however take leave for the present of the public capacity of Sir SAMUEL SHEPHERD with one observation, which applies, in some degree, to his private character, and affords an additional reason why he is still widely respected and esteemed. In all his thoughts and actions he seems to be perfectly a gentleman ; in all the prosecutions he has conducted, he has behaved towards the parties with fairness and liberality ; he has displayed sometimes a degree of candour quite unusual and unexpected, and has made admissions that did him credit but his cause injury. I a defendant stood on the floor to vindicate himself, I do not think it can be truly said of Sir SAMUEL SHEPHERD that he ever attempted to avail himself unduly of the power and influence of his station, either with the Jury or the Court: he never assumed any authoritative and overbearing deportment, or attempted to dictate, as his predecessors have been allowed to do, the course of proceeding. Yet his temper sustained many severe trials, and as far as I witnessed it, his conduct set an example of forbearance not always followed by the Court.

Of the Attorney-General's talents I do not think so highly, whether he exercise them as an advocate in or out of Parliament. His deafness has much increased upon him within the memory of several of the younger sergeants who have profited by it. It has been of long continuance, but it is the opinion of those who remember Sir SAMUEL SHEPHERD in his younger days, that he was an able advocate and an eloquent speaker: my acquaintance with Courts of Justice does not go quite so far back, but I well recollect him when his

deafness was comparatively slight and tempo
rary; and though I might then consider hir
shrewd and sensible, I never once imagine
that he was eloquent. I have seen him in ver
nearly all the Government prosecutions I
has conducted or aided since he obtaine
his appointments as Solicitor and afterward
as Attorney-General, and I am very positiv
that my first impression was correct. H
defect of hearing, and the quantity of snuff h
takes, have undoubtedly injured his voice
which was once clear, though not musical nc
round in its tones; but had he ever been elc
quent it could but little, if at all, impede th
impetuous current of his thoughts and words
the flow, when it amounts to a continue
stream, is uniformly meagre, and generall
irregular: it has neither force, fulness, deptl
nor dignity; when he strives to appear im
passioned, he is only inflated, and all hi
exertions to be eloquent are more or less vapi
and unsubstantial. This remark applies t
the attempts at declamation which he feel
it necessary to make when he is managing a
important public prosecution. *Cum omni*

arrogantia odiosa est, **tum illa ingenii et elo-
quentiæ multo molestissima,** and if he have
not precisely what we mean by the arrogance,
he has at least a good deal of the pretence of
eloquence.　To give him his proper character,
he is a clear-headed, straight-forward gentlemanly speaker, and if he is occasionally impressive, particularly in his manner, he most
commonly injudiciously wastes his energy
and emphasis upon matters that require them
least.　His sentences are not confused, but
they are shapeless, and often turgid and
laborious.

His action is unusually vehement upon all
occasions, whether it is or is not required :
he resorts to the ordinary expedient of making
up for the weakness of his language, by the
strength of his corporeal exertions.　I do not
mean that he throws about his figure in all
directions, as Mr. Marryat does, like a por-
poise in a storm, for he keeps that uncommonly erect ; the motion is confined principally to his arms and feet.　His deafness
prevents him from properly regulating his

voice, and fearing when he is strenuousl
endeavouring to enforce a particular poin
that he shall speak too loud, his words be
come almost inaudible, while his arms an
hands are employed in striking the desk o
table with so much violence, that the whol
Court resounds. The effect is rendered sti
more ludicrous by his rising upon his toes t
give his small person importance, and beal
ing time with his heels upon the floor.
well remember during Hone's trial, upon on
occasion in particular, when the Attorney
General was endeavouring to declaim agains
profanation, the proceeding was interrupte
by the indecorous laughter of the spectator
and commitments were properly threatene
in consequence by the Judge; but the laught
was not occasioned by what was said, but b
the manner of saying it. This I mentio
merely as an illustration, for the defect :
chiefly, if not altogether, to be attributed t
the infirmity under which Sir SAMUEL SHEI
HERD has unfortunately so long laboured.

Few men have obtained much business i

the profession of the Law, without possessing
a share of talent of some kind, or some information beyond their competitors; and I am
inclined to think that Sir S. SHEPHERD, when
young, combined considerable acuteness with
great industry and discretion; it is certain
that his practice in the Common Pleas was
once as extensive, or more extensive, than
that of any of his rivals; and he was often
employed in causes, which such men as
Mr. Sergeant Best or Mr. Sergeant Vaughan
could have no pretensions to touch—I mean
those where legal research and learning where
required.   The Attorney-General bears the
reputation of being a very well-read man in
the higher departments of his pursuit; and
as far as I am able to judge he deserves the
character.   This qualification probably recommended him first to the notice of Ministers as Solicitor-General, at a time when they
had an Attorney-General, who throughout his
life had substituted a profound knowledge of
human nature in its depravity, for a knowledge of the most ordinary books.   It is
thought, notwithstanding, by some lawyers,
that Sir S. SHEPHERD, as opposed to Sir

V. Gibbs, failed in the great legal contes
between Sir F. Burdett and the Speaker o
the House of Commons. In point of law
however, I am afraid he had the worst sid
of the argument.

It would be extremely unfair to form an
judgment of his capability to examine a
adverse witness, from any attempt he ma
at present make: in fact, be loses half th
important parts of the testimony—the littl
niceties on which credit depends, and which
if seized and pressed home, would shew tha
the person in the box was unworthy of be
lief. Judging as well as I can from recollec
tion, from the report of those who have know
the Bar longer, and from the partial succes
of some of his more recent exertions of thi
kind, I should be inclined to think that h
acquired a portion of his former eminenc
by his talent in this department of the pro
vince of an advocate.

Of his abilities, as a parliamentary debate
little notion can be formed by those in th

gallery of the House of Commons but from inference; for he is seldom audible beyond the benches surrounding him. He is not required to speak but upon legal questions, which have been more numerous than usual within the last two or three sessions. His addresses are very inefficient, and draw but few cheers even from those who are most interested in encouraging him. Sir W. Garrow generally obtained his greatest applause from his antagonists, who of course received with shouts the sentences in which he committed himself, and destroyed his own positions. This is an error into which the present Attorney-General is too prudent to be likely to fall; but if he did, the smallness of his voice would frequently enable him to do it with impunity.

SIR ARTHUR PIGGOT.

IT is generally remarked in the profession
that the Chancery is the most gentlemanly
of all the courts: this epithet requires ex
planation:—a learned court or an impartia
court would be intelligible, but few person
would understand precisely what is intende
by a *gentlemanly* court of law or equity
Some might suppose that it meant a plac
where most money is gained by the lea
labour, and a barrister consequently soone
acquires the property of a gentleman ; th
fact however is otherwise : others might fanc

that it meant a court where none but individuals of a certain station in society practise; but this would also be incorrect; while a third party might imagine that it was composed of men, who in the ordinary intercourse of life conducted themselves with greater decorum and propriety. I am not aware however that in this respect the counsel in one court have much, if any, advantage over those of another. In Chancery there is certainly not so much low business requiring a knowledge of mean legal artifices, and therefore particular individuals may be excluded; but as a body they are pretty nearly upon an equality, and perhaps in all the courts some might be pointed out who have resorted to all kinds of despicable expedients and base contrivances to get into the good graces of the attornies; who have practised the art of *hugging* with complete success—who have secured business by invitations to dinner—by well-timed presents of fish or game—by hearty and unseen shakes of the hand in the street, which they dared not have given in Westminster-Hall, and by all those ingenuous means, to which

men of great talent have before now conde-
scended, and by which men of little talent
have sometimes gained considerable fortunes.

The difference however between the Chancery and other courts consists more in the
mode in which the business is transacted than
in the nature of the business itself, or the
means by which it has been procured ; and
this distinction is owing less to the Bar than
to the Bench.   The Court is gentlemanly, because the judge is a gentleman : for there
perhaps never was a man who presided in
such a situation with more suavity and urbanity than Lord ELDON—who more effectually endeavoured to fore-shorten the distance
between the Bench and the Bar—who listened
with more patience to the observations of
counsel on all sides, and whose chief fault
arises from a painfully anxious desire to have
no fault.   Of course I here separate his judicial from his political capacity ; for I ap-
plaud the first just as highly as I reprobate
the last, and on this account my tribute will
at least be thought to have the merit of since-

ity. He is considered, and rightly, one of the ablest Chancellors ever intrusted with the great seal, and his natural disposition, as far as an opinion can be formed of it in public, seems to be as kind and amiable as his mind is well instructed in the learning of his profession. He listens with equal patience to the oldest and to the youngest counsel; and suitors who are unable or unwilling to employ advocates are never impetuously dismissed unheard. His Lordship, on one occasion, declared that it was the duty of a judge to devote his utmost attention to persons in such a predicament: and that he who even needlessly interrupted them, much more repelled them with unfeeling and coarse brutality, was unworthy of the office confided to him.* This mild and tranquil deportment—this gentlemanly ease—cannot have been displayed by Lord Eldon, for more than sixteen years, without producing a corresponding

* In the case of Thomas Nias, a bankrupt, who put Lord Eldon's resignation to the test, for he made an address to His Lordship, which occupied the greater part of two days, and consisted of the most minute details.

feeling among the advocates in his Court : business is transacted with all the pleasantness of somewhat restrained private friendship. In Chancery there is little need to impose upon the suitors or the public by any assumed gravity or dignity ; and the individual who now presides appears to walk upon the exact line between haughty pomposity and degrading familiarity. This is what is meant by the word *gentlemanly,* as applied to the Court of Chancery.

It has been before remarked, that low sharp practice, and its followers, are in some measure excluded : and the mode in which matters are brought before the Lord Chancellor contributes to preserve more decorum, both of speech and conduct, than usually prevails in Courts of Law : the proceedings are chiefly conducted in writing by bills, answers, affidavits, &c. so that there are no *vivâ voce* examinations, no badgering and bullying of witnesses, and no personal disputes among counsel as to what has or has not been established ; for if a difference of that kind arise it is here easily settled by an appeal to the instrument itself : this makes advocates less bold and broad in their assertions, and it is easy to see how in various respects these *literæ scriptæ*, disadvantageous in many other ways, tend to moderate and refine the proceedings of a court, whose decisions, by its constitution, do not depend upon the personal interrogation of individuals.

It must be obvious notwithstanding that this very gentlemanliness, chiefly occasioned by the unassuming unpretending conduct of the Judge, may very materially interfere with the progress and display of any thing like eloquence. Sir Samuel Romilly is almost the only man who has shewn in the Court of Chancery that he possesses it : Mr. Fonblanque is a clear and a clever speaker, when his friends afford him an opportunity, and Mr. Montague can talk loud and long—can refer to a sentence or two from Lord Bacon (about the only author I ever heard him quote) and mouth a polysyllable word with most emphatic want of meaning: but he has seldom

been thought really eloquent by any body
but himself. I am now speaking of eloquenc
in the ordinary sense in which the word i
understood, and in which it is used by on
of our best poets, when he speaks of the

> Power above powers, heavenly eloquence!
>   That with the strong reign of commanding words
> Doth manage, guide, and master th' eminence
> Of men's affections more than all their swords.
>
>   *S. Daniel's Musophilus.*

Some may urge that I have laid too much
stress upon it, and seem to hold it a matter of
too great importance; they may say that
in considering the qualifications of any particular counsel, I ought not first to ask mysel
whether he be or be not eloquent: that I ought
rather to weigh the solidity of his understanding and sound the depth of his learning: on
they may contend that I take eloquence in
too restrained a signification; that it has at
least too kinds; the declamatory and the
argumentative, and that the latter is by far
the most useful and valuable. It is true that
there are not only two, but perhaps twenty

I

other sorts and sub-divisions of eloquence, all excellent in their way, but all secondary to that referred to in the above quotation, as having power to guide and master man's strongest and fiercest passions. Owen Felham, drawing a distinction between the poet and the orator, says, "that he is the best orator that pleases most;" and admitting the distinction, what species of oratory or eloquence is most generally approved?

I certainly do not bring forward Sir ARTHUR PIGGOT, in the present article, as an individual possessing this highest qualification of an advocate, but because his general talents and acquirements and his long standing, as the senior king's counsel at the Chancery Bar, seem to entitle him to be first noticed: not indeed that I have considered myself at all bound by this rule; because, for the sake of convenience, contrast, or for the purpose of enforcing some particular point, it has sometimes appeared proper to dispense with it. I do not know any man who practises in the same Court, who has less pretensions to any thing ap-

proaching the ornaments of rhetoric : his eloquence is entirely of the argumentative kind,
and even here he has considerable defects and
deficiencies, as will be shewn presently. It
is to be remarked, that in equity all that is
very important to an advocate is a knowledge
of his business, a distinct mode of detailing
facts, and a perspicuous manner of stating
arguments founded upon them : eloquence,
or any attempts at it beyond a clear uninter-
rupted flow of words and thoughts, would on
most occasions be wasted. The counsel do
not address a jury of twelve men upon matters
with which their individual feelings may be
connected, but a single judge of great experience, who has long learnt to subdue and
controul ordinary impulses, and whose principal business it is to determine according to
precedent. It has been said that a judge
should be without passions, but whether he
ought or ought not to be influenced by them
on the Bench, few would suppose that the
matters commonly brought before the Lord
Chancellor are of a nature likely to excite
them. Yet to a certain degree this is a mis-

ake, partly originating perhaps in the sati-
rical attack of the late Mr. Windham :* how
can it be said that subjects interesting to the
feelings do not come before the individual
who superintends all the charitable institu-
tions of the country, and upon whose decisions, in lunacy and bankruptcy only, frequently depend the liberties, fortunes, and
almost the lives of men. Surely here is a
field extensive enough for the employment
of all the powers of language ; but the gentlemanliness, before referred to, interferes and
cramps exertion ; besides which it may admit of considerable doubt, whether by a man
like Lord Eldon, justice is not more effec-
ually administered, without any effort to
mislead his understanding, and pervert his
judgment, by rousing his sensibility. The
occasions are therefore extremely rare where

* In his celebrated speech on the Walcheren expedi-
on ; the only set address I had the delight of hearing him
make, and which, from some pique between him and the
reporters, I believe never found its way into the newspapers. It is not easy to see how the two subjects were
connected, nor can I recollect now exactly how that most
ingenious man employed one to illustrate the other.

eloquence is required, and still rarer where it is displayed. The secondary sort of eloquence however, that which consists in argumentative and reasoning powers is indispensable, and the possession of this faculty, though not perhaps in its perfection, long secured to Sir ARTHUR PIGGOT the leading practice in this Court. Of late his business has somewhat declined, or perhaps he has declined his business, as his advanced age now prevents him from undergoing the fatigues he formerly could endure. He is perhaps the most of any man at this Bar an exception to the gentlemanliness for which it is celebrated, for his ordinary stile of speaking is homely and rude, sometimes sufficiently strenuous, but hard, blunt, and crude, apparently without the slightest wish to display any of the graces of delivery. His voice too corresponds with his stile of speaking, for it is harsh and unmusical in its tones, and without modulation or inflection.

Although Sir ARTHUR PIGGOT's chief excellence consists in his reasoning powers, he is by no means a good arguer of a question : he can enforce a particular topic with con- iderable vehemence and effect—he can bring o bear upon it all the facts supplied, and he can state those facts with precision and clear- ness—yet he never seems to contemplate more han this single point : he does not carry on he chain of his reasoning from one thing to another until he has encircled the whole case : he exhausts himself upon a particular part, and when he is obliged to advert to others, he repeats much of what he has before said, and in nearly the same terms as those he be- ore used.   He seems to want a logical head, which arranges and constructs an argument with the same attention to proportion and elation of parts, as an architect constructs a building.   Some men, when they read the most complicated cases, dispose of all the parts in their fit places as they proceed, ac- cording to the conclusions at which they are desirous of arriving : in time it becomes almost a mechanical habit with them; but Sir A. PIGGOT, with all his practice, seems never o have acquired any facility of this kind, so

that his speeches are often a jumble and confused mass of things excellent in their proper
places, and if duly supported, but having
little strength or force standing alone, and in
the situation where they are found : he frequently begins where he ought to end, and
ends where he ought to begin, while the middle of his speech is made up of scraps of
repetition of arguments, and re-statement of
trifling details. This defect originated no
doubt in the too great abundance of his
business at one time, and the absence of the
faculty of what may be termed *extempore*
arrangement. It has perhaps increased upon
him of late, but I apprehend that it was
always more or less prevalent, and, as a recent
instance, his address upon the subject of the
affairs of Drury-Lane Theatre may be referred to.

It will be easily imagined that a man who
takes so little pains about his speaking will
take less about his action : he scarcely employs any at all, but most commonly stands
quite erect, and delivers his words as Fria

Bacon's brazen head would be supposed to have done : he looks more like an automaton than a living creature, and never directs his eyes towards the individual he *is* addressing, but speaks directly at the Lord Chancellor's *insignia* of office, as if they only ought to receive his special attention. Yet he seems to see nothing, and never moves his arms, excepting to take up his brief and lay it down again without examination. His extensive knowledge of his profession, the earnestness he usually displays in the cause in which he is engaged, the respect paid by the Bench to his judgment, and the faculty he enjoys of dwelling upon and enforcing separate points, and those commonly of the greatest consequence, secured him for a long series of years the first business of the Court.

There is one peculiarity about his stile of speaking which I omitted to notice, and which induces me to think that he would have had considerable success as a *nisi prius* advocate in some of the other Courts. When attorney-general, he had little to do with

public prosecutions, nor do I recollect seeing
him conduct any of them ; but the shortness
of his sentences in speaking, and his colloquial, interrogatory manner, would be better
adapted to produce an effect upon a jury
than to convince a judge : it rather obstructs
than aids the course of a legal argument,
which does not require any great terseness,
or sharpness of expression. There is, too,
about the frame of Sir ARTHUR PIGGOT's
mind an acuteness and shrewdness that would
have enabled him to examine witnesses with
success. At the same time, his monotony
and want of action might have been injurious ;
but I am not sure if both have not been occasioned, or at any rate increased, by a fear
n his part lest his energy, of which he ha:
a large share, should too far o'erstep the
decorum of this Court.

THE SOLICITOR GENERAL.

Siker, now I see thou speakest of spite
All for thou lackest some deal his delight;
I, as I am, had rather be envied,
All were it of my foe, than fondly pitied.
Sp. Shep. Cal. for May.

IF, as was shewn when speaking of the Attorney-General, " of all offices in the gift of the Crown that of Attorney-General is least to be coveted," that of Solicitor-General is perhaps most to be desired. In point of rank the latter is but just inferior to the former, and the Solicitor-General is relieved from a great part of the weight of public odium which his coadjutor is under the necessity of sustaining. The Attorney-General stands forward, almost alone, as the public spy, informer, and prosecutor: all *ex-officio* informations against the libellers of his patrons, or other supposed delinquents, are filed in his name, and the wrath of the parties, and their supporters, and the dislike of the nation at large, are levelled principally against him, while the Solicitor-General fights under his shield and sometimes appears not to enter into the contest at all; if he assist in any public proceeding, by far the larger portion of labour and ostensibility belongs to his leader and superior.

It is an error, too, to suppose, that the Solicitor-General has much more official business to transact. I mean much more of that business which is managed within doors and out of sight: he may, and probably does, lend his aid in considering whether such and such a production be or be not libellous, in cases where the advice of their law officers is required by Ministers; but he has no more to do with the fagging drudgery, which is supposed to belong to his situation, than the Attorney-General. It is not commonly known, that there is a subordinate individual connected with the offices of both, who in the profession is called by the *Nick*-name of a

much-injured infernal personage, whose dut
it is to go through all, or nearly all, th
labour, for a comparatively small part of th
emolument—with however, sometimes, a soi
of implied promise that if he is zealous in th
cause and renders himself useful, when th
opportunity occurs, and he *is* no longe
wanted, he shall be made a puisne Judge, o
allowed some other "honourable retirement."
How long, exactly, this practice has prevaile
I know not, but this under-scrub is paid b
the public, and though not ministerial
avowed, is ministerially employed. It i
understood that Mr. Richardson, a man o
great learning and experience, is the presen
devil, and it is his duty to draw or settle al
informations, indictments, or other forms o
proceedings emanating from the office of At
torney-General.* Thus the odium that migh
otherwise attach to the Solicitor-General, i
diminished by the ostensibility of the Attorney
General, and his labours, are lessened by thei
mutual assistant—the *devil*.

K

* Since the above was first written he has been eleva
ted to the Bench : See the Criticism upon him in a sub
sequent page.

It is not surprising therefore that so young a man as Sir ROBERT GIFFORD, (or at least a man so young in the profession) should be willing to accept the emoluments and honours of such an appointment; nor is it to be wondered that by so doing he should have drawn upon himself the envy and animosity of a few whose standing and higher rank in the law seemed to give them a prior claim: I say whose standing and higher rank seemed to give them a prior claim, because certainly in most other respects Sir ROBERT GIFFORD was equal to any man at the Bar. Bitter indeed must have been the mortification of some, who having spent a long life in patient servility, and industrious flattery, thus saw their hopes disappointed, their exertions misapplied, and their submission and fawning only contributing to render them contemptible to the world, and despicable even to themselves. It afforded also a useful lesson to the younger aspirants who were following, or preparing to follow the same course. That Ministers however deserved credit for this appointment, on the score of impartiality, ought not to be admitted: it was an act rather of necessity than of choice, for they were, not without reason, tired of nominating men by whose ignorance and arrogance they had been severe sufferers, to whose judgment they could not trust, and on whose prudence they could not rely. In accepting the office, this praise is due to the Solicitor-General, as well as to his colleague, that he did not disgrace himself by deserting the principles he had through life maintained, though in the first instance those principles might have been settled or influenced by some consideration of his future success.

In his public legal capacity the Solicitor General has yet come forward upon few occasions: he lent his aid, trifling as it necessarily was, on the trials of Hone, but he was not present when Wooler resisted the two *ex officio* informations filed against him. In the proceeding against Preston, Thistlewood, and others, for high treason, he most distinguished himself; the speech he made in summing up the case for the Crown realized all the expectations of his friends, and the hopes of his patrons, while it gave his rivals and enemies an

opportunity of seeing that he was quite equal
to the arduous duty for which they wished
he might prove incompetent. At that time
he had just made a sudden and unexampled
leap from the fourth or fifth row behind the
bar, to one of the most exalted stations connected with the profession: the eyes of all
parties were fixed upon him, and even high
talents and attainments might have sunk under
the appalling embarrassments and difficulties;
but the magnitude of the question, and the
greatness of his stake, only seemed to rouse in
him new energies, and to call forth additional
firmness. His address was one of the most
luminous in point of arrangement, forcible in
point of argument, and correct in point of delivery, that had ever been heard in the King's
Bench. The effect of it was encreased by
the feebleness of the narrative attempted by
the Attorney-General in his opening, who
notwithstanding his great experience, in the
amiable diffidence of his nature seemed to feel
that he was unequal to the task he had undertaken. I do not mean to imply that Sir
ROBERT GIFFORD has not a sufficient share

of self-mistrust, but at such a time it would
have been misplaced, when the weakness of the
individual might have been mistaken for the
weakness of the cause. This is almost the
only instance in which the talents of the Soli
citor-General have been publicly put to the
test in London, for though in the country he
was rapidly rising into business, and was
entrusted with the management of some most
important cases, yet in the metropolis, and
with its inhabitants at large, he had yet to
establish his reputation: among lawyers his
abilities and his learning were never doubted
from the first, and although his elevation was
not expected to be so early, it was considered
eventually certain. Hitherto his practice in
Westminster-hall had been confined to questions of legal nicety and subtlety, and especially to those relating to the dark and complicated subject of real property, to which some
men have devoted their whole study, and
whose business it has seemed still further to
involve it in new intricacies, and to encumber

it with fresh absurdities.* With such men
as the laborious and mindless Sugden and
Preston, Sir R. GIFFORD has not unfrequently
been matched, against them he has had to
measure the depth of his learning, and the
strength of his reasoning, and if not the best of
the argument, (which of course must depend
upon other circumstances,) he has always
had the best argument; in learning he at least
seemed equal, and in all other respects superior. In fact though Sir ROBERT GIFFORD
has only been a few years at the Bar, if I am
not mistaken he practised under it for some
time, and the intensity and steadiness of his
application are almost proverbial; above all
he possesses a logical head, endowed with the
rare faculty of arranging all its acquisitions;
the furniture is not only solid, but disposed
in the best order, so that with the aid of a retentive memory, his knowledge is all applicable even upon emergencies. Others could

---

* A great lawyer has called it a beautiful system, and
it is so for lawyers; at least half the emoluments of the
profession are derived from disputes and arrangements
regarding real property.

be named, (such for instance as his antagonist last above mentioned) who possesses most extensive information, but they are a mere chaos of learning, confounded by confusion : they have

—————————Skill that doth poduce
But terms and tongues and parrating of art—
That which some call a learned ignorance ;
A serious trifle, error in a trance.

G. Chapman's Euthymiæ Raptus.

Besides his great learning not only upon real property questions, but upon those relating to commerce and shipping, and besides his admirable mode of employing his knowledge, few men at the Bar enjoy greater quickness and readiness than the Solicitor General—few men seize a point with equal rapidity, or illustrate it with more effect. I never saw him conduct a cause at *Nisi Prius* in London, but in the country several, and his acuteness as well as his prudence were surprising. I must nevertheless deny him the highest qualification of an advocate ; he has not the natural gift of eloquence, though he has acquired great facility in the use of language: his attempts to rouse the feelings, or to influence the understandings of his hearers, were commonly feeble; but he seldom attempted any thing of the kind, and his deficiency in this respect is much counterbalanced by other admirable requisites: for instance, if Sir ROBERT GIFFORD be not eloquent, he is one of the clearest and most perspicuous speakers ever heard: his voice is peculiarly distinct, though inharmonious, and his sentences are usually complete, though not formed with any great nicety or art: he probably never studied style, but the distinct view he himself takes of a case, is sure to meet with a corresponding distinctness of statement: the facts are always arranged so as to shew their bearings upon each other, and what with others would generally be a mere detail, is by him so artfully managed, that it is really an argument in favour of the side he supports: his audience is, therefore, always gratified, if not delighted. He is a skilful pilot of what is called an unseaworthy case, and sometimes brings it into port in safety, in spite of its own rottenness, and of all the winds and waves of

opposition. His examinations of witnesse:
are marked by penetration, sagacity, and
acuteness.

He has been spoken of hitherto as a counse
before a jury; but since his appointment a:
Solicitor-General, he has changed his Court
and now confines his private practice exclusively to Equity : notwithstanding the excel
lence of his general management of an actio:
at law, I do not think that the change is to b
regretted : in the first place, (a matter perhap
of little consequence) in Chancery the Soli
citor-General is at his constitutional post, an
(what is of more importance) it will be see:
that his peculiar merits and qualifications ar
such as to be most useful in that Court, whe:
eloquence is little needed, and where a cohe
rent and perspicuous statement of circum
stances, with the arguments resulting fror
them, is much more essential. His busines
of late has very much increased, and, speak
ing generally, it is impossible that it shoul
be done better.

There is little to be said of the external man

ner of Sir ROBERT GIFFORD, while speaking;
he uses little or no action, but his style does
not require it ; or if it did, the expressiveness
of his countenance (not always amiable) and
the ejaculations of his intelligent and full
black eye would amply supply the deficiency.
His general appearance is thoughtful and
meditative, with very little of that superficial
and skin-deep quickness which usually de-
notes an absence of sounder qualities.   At the
same time he looks far from a good-tempered
man, and as he resembles Sir V. Gibbs very
much in the qualities of his mind and in his
mode of conducting matters entrusted to him,
he rivals him also, in some degree, in the
peevishness and pettishness he displays when
slight and unexpected obstacles occur, or
when those who give him his instructions do
not accord with his views, or are too slow of
apprehension to understand them.

Regarding his speeches in the House of
Commons it may be fit to add a word or two :
some persons who, excepting that their minds
are probably slightly tinctured with envy,

would be deemed pretty competent judges, think that here at least he has failed. I am not of that opinion, for he has done all that ought to have been expected from him. At most of the few debates in which he has taken part, I was present : the questions were generally purely legal, and his arguments were as usual clear, ingenious, and forcible : they certainly had the fault of a want of enlargement in the views taken of the subject, but this error is common to nearly every lawyer that ever spoke in the Senate : it is an error arising out of their education and habits, not out of any actual difference in the construction of their minds : and it is surely a little too much to ask that he who is so absolute a lawyer in Court should not be a lawyer in Parliament.*

* I feel it a matter of fairness to allow that some of Sir R. Gifford's late efforts in the House of Commons, even upon legal questions, have not been so successful either in convincing the members or, of course, in pleasing his patrons as the speeches he had delivered before the above article was first printed—at the same time they did not betray so much a want of knowledge as a want of temper. He now fills the office of Attorney-General, Sir S. Shepherd having been removed to a judicial station in Scotland.

It may be thought that in this criticism I have been a little too partial: it may be so, and I confess that ever since Sir ROBERT GIFFORD first came forward he has been a growing favourite with me.

MR. TOPPING.

A partial praise shall never elevate
  My settled censure of my own esteem ;
A cankered verdict of malignant hate
  Shall ne'er provoke me worse myself to deem ;
Spite of despite, and rancour's villany
I am myself————

John Marston's Scourge of Villany.

THERE are few abuses at the Bar more crying
at the present moment than the mode in
which the examination ef witnesses is sometimes conducted ; of course no reference is
here intended to the technical rules of evidence so long established, and to which perhaps few objections can be reasonably made,
but to the manner in which Counsel are per-
mitted to overstep all the bounds of decorum
and propriety in their interrogatories. Instances could be pointed out where female
delicacy has been outraged with unfeeling

wontonness, and the most innocent witness is often so confounded by the novelty of his situation, and so bewildered by rapid and purposely complicated questions, that he is absolutely entrapped into falsehood and perjury : under such circumstances the caution of the Satirist can be of no avail :——

> ————————ambiguæ si quando citabere testis
> Incertæque rei, Phalaris licet imperet ut sis
> Falsus, &c.

A witness might be proof against all bodily torture, though not against the unfair and even despicable artifices employed to cheat him into a declaration of what is untrue : he may enter the box with a resolution to tell a plain straight-forward story, and to adhere closely to facts within his own knowledge; but if he be not a man of more than ordinary firmness and acuteness, his purpose will be defeated by those who have attained such skill in confusing what is clear, and involving what is simple. The offence offered to the diffidence and delicacy of women, so frequently and so needlessly, though interfering with the due administration of justice, is com-

paratively a minor evil, and most commonly
but a part of the same system. I have mor
than once had occasion to speak of the power
and penetrating sagacity of Sir W. Garrow
in managing the examination of an advers
witness, and though true it is that he was sel
dom very scrupulous as to the mode in which
he extracted or confounded truth, and though
he had as much coarseness and as little feeling
as any man who ever practised, yet he seldom
without some cause or other broke through
the ordinary rules of decorum and politeness
if he did so, it usually turned out that the
individual he was perforating by his dogged
interrogatories deserved the treatment he received. While he continued at the Bar he
was justly considered unrivalled in this respect, and few men, not even those of the
highest rank, ventured to put themselves in
competition; but since his elevation to the
Bench there is scarcely a single Counsel, however young and inexperienced, who does not
think himself warranted in going all lengths,
and this frequently without any instructions
to warrant an attack upon the character and

demeanour of the witness : all flatter themselves that they are peculiarly gifted, and
take every opportunity of shewing how much
they are deceived in their self-conceited estimate.   To such an extent has this abuse been
carried, that of late it has sometimes called
for the controuling power of the Bench, which
finds that the discretion generally allowed to
Sir W. Garrow ought not to be entrusted
to his overweening imitators.

It has often excited astonishment that a
shrewd and practised Advocate should be
disconcerted, if not dumb-foundered, by an
answer in the spirit of his question, or by a
retort remarkable only for its impertinence or
effrontery ; but the wonder ends the moment
we reflect, that those who may be most accustomed to attack, on that account may be
least competent to defend, and that Counsel,
covered by their imposing paraphernalia,
only prepare themselves to assail : they fight
as it were with a long sword, by which they
keep their antagonist (who they take care
shall be unarmed and as helpless as possible)

at a distance; but if he have resolution to
advance, or the skill to meet them at their
own weapon, as they have only learnt to
thrust and not to parry, they are compelled
to retire or submit. This is the true cause of
the constant appeals made by Counsel to the
Court, when they happen to encounter an individual who makes even a faint attempt at
retaliation.

Some of the foregoing remarks will apply
to the gentleman who is the subject of the
present article, and who is the senior practising Counsel in the Court of King's Bench:
in the outset however let me relieve him from
the supposed charge of intentionally and unnecessarily infringing upon the delicacy and
consideration due to female witnesses: I never
observed it, nor have I ever heard that he
was guilty of such an offence. Of course
however, his standing at the Bar warrants him
in taking upon himself as much or more
license than any of his present competitors
and it must be allowed that he generally
avails himself of his privilege, though not al

ways to the advantage of his clients; for it is obvious that if an Advocate severely cross-examine a witness and totally fail, the Jury, to a certain extent, must feel disgusted, and the cause will probably suffer in proportion. Mr. Topping may be, and no doubt is, like other men, sometimes misinstructed, but one of his great faults is, that he never seems to endeavour to judge of the correctness of the instructions put into his hands by the Attorney, by watching closely the demeanour and appearance of the witness: he is an industrious pains-taking note-maker of all the deposition in chief, or what the witness proves for the party on whose behalf he is called, but instead of poring over his pen and keeping his eyes invariably fixed upon his brief, he should be minutely scrutinizing the conduct and countenance of the person in the box: he should leave to his younger co-adjutor the labour of taking notes; for all men who have been successful in this department of the office of an Advocate, have been much more careless about what a witness said than about the manner in which it was said—the general appear-

ance and the various expressions of the face :
every body knows that there is no interrogatory so effectual in detecting guilt as that
which is put by a steady and searching eye;
a man who is skilful in this respect will keep
up a sort of silent cross-examination of a person, all the time he is giving evidence for the
opposite party. Not a few of the awkward
dilemmas into which Mr. Topping has at various times fallen, are to be attributed to his
constant. neglect of this mode of detecting
falsehood ; the questions he puts are generally framed with sufficient ingenuity, and long
practice has given him a knack, which men of
greater quickness do not always attain, viz.
that of ever having a second question ready to
follow up the first, and to stifle the answer to
the first, provided that answer do not exactly
suit his purpose. This expedient is, notwithstanding, held a little unfair, and is frequently exclaimed against, though all more or less
pursue it according to the degree of facility
they have acquired.

Mr. Topping is also not remarkable for the

gentlemanliness of the mode in which he conducts an examination.   I have acquitted him
of all design to insult or outrage female delicacy, but at the same time it cannot be denied
that there is a coarseness and even a vulgarity in his language and manner that are liable
to misinterpretation: this is aided by the grat-
ing hoarseness of his voice.*   His words are
usually unselected, and if there be a mild and
a harsh way of putting a question, he does
not give himself the trouble to consider which
will be least offensive; yet if he receive an
answer, partly called for by the terms of the
question, his indignation instantly rises and
he usually appeals to the Court against this
uncalled-for insolence.   He appears to think
that a witness is bound to endure all and to

* The following epigrammatic description of the
voices of the four leading counsel of the Court of King's
Bench was handed about among the younkers a year or
two ago :—
    " Scarlet neighs like a stallion, and Marryat
    " Barks out his short words like a dog ;
    " Gurney looks like and talks like a parrot ;
    " Topping croaks between raven and frog."
This is of course not given because it is by any means
true to the full extent, but because it is sufficiently true
to be characteristic.

return nothing; though, considering the extent of his practice, there is no Counsel who has been so frequently interrupted by the Bench with a sort of gentle hint that more restraint would be becoming. I have some reluctance in making these remarks upon Mr. Topping, however just, because I understand and believe, that in private life he is a man of peculiarly kind and gentlemanly deportment, and it only shews that the sort of masquerade in which the persons of Counsel appear in public, makes them sometimes put their thoughts and feelings in masquerade also; not a few are very different beings with very different natures, when they put off their legal habiliments.

The practice enjoyed by Mr. TOPPING has fluctuated much since he became King's Counsel, about twelve or thirteen years ago: for a considerable time he sat briefless within the Bar at Westminster, excepting when his aid was required in a case from the Northern Circuit, where he had some business; and I do not hesitate to say that for the greater part of his emoluments he is more indebted to his good fortune than to his talents : though *tutius est fictis contendere verbis*, yet, as far as relates to promotion and advancement, the law resembles the army, since it much depends upon stepping into dead men's shoes; if I mistake not Mr. TOPPING obtained the greater share of his business in the country on the death of Mr. Sergeant Cockell, after which he and Mr. Justice Park long kept the lead, not so much because they merited the station, as because there were then no Barristers of sufficient rank and standing to oppose them. Circumstances in a similar manner combined in his favour in London, for the elevation of Sir V. Gibbs, threw many briefs unavoidably into his hands, and made him for some time a competitor, however unequal, with Sir W. Garrow : at that period, to use a vulgar phrase, there was little more than Hobson's choice, Mr. TOPPING or nobody,—(that is to say, Mr. Park,)—to oppose Sir W. Garrow. Within the last three or four years however about six or eight new silk-gowns have been given away in the King's Bench, and the consequence has been, that Mr. TOPPING's

usiness has much declined: it has fallen
hiefly into the hands of younger rivals,
Iessrs. Scarlett, Marryat, and Gurney. This
ct therefore proves the correctness of what I
.dvanced, that Mr. Topping would not have
l een nearly so often employed but for a few
fortuitous coincidences.

It has been already stated that Mr. Topping
an industrious pains-taking man, who reads
nis instructions patiently, and adheres to them
faithfully: his other merits are however neither numerous nor prominent. Of late his
health has certainly suffered, and to that his
friends have mainly attributed the decay of his
practice: he no longer possesses much of that
temporary energy which I used formerly to
think his principal recommendation. His
speech, in opening a case was always the worst
part of his mode of conducting it: if the facts
were numerous and complicated, the laborious
reading he had given his brief appeared to
entangle and confuse him; and by stating
and restating the same thing, he usually required twice as much time as would have

been necessary for a combined and concen-
trated detail; not that his memory was defective, but he failed in putting things in their
right place. The articulation of his words
is always indistinct, arising partly perhaps
from an attempt to smother and conceal his
strong northern accent ; and though his voice
is naturally strong, he seldom throws it out,
as if he were afraid of betraying its harshness.
In the North I have heard his Yorkshire
brogue (if it my be so called) of considerable
use to him ; but it is much to be regretted that
he could never leave much of it behind him.

Judging from what is seen of it in public,
it would be said that Mr. TOPPING's temper
now and then requires great regulation ; he is
much too irritable on slight and unintentional
interruptions : he has sometimes appeared as
it were overwhelmed in the foam of his own
wrath, but when it has subsided a little, it
gives him an impulse which displays his
temporary energy to advantage : it gives rise
to two or three vigorous sentences which tell
with the Jury, and if they be a little too
much ornamented with Friar John's *Couleurs*

de rhetorique Ciceroniane, they may be admitted in the absence of something better; they have their effect upon those who mistake constitutional heat for the passion of eloquence. His action, like Mr. Marryat's, is confined generally to his head and shoulders, though he now and then doubles his fist very imposingly. His face, never very inviting, when he is angry is grievously distorted even to ferocity : his own witnesses are frequently terror-struck.

Though a man of much experience in routine business, he is not looked upon in the profession as a man of much learning. His general information seems to lie in a narrow compass ; or if it be at all extensive, he is one of a number who make but little use of their acquirements in a situation where every species of knowledge may be turned to account. Upon the whole, I am inclined to think that Mr. TOPPING is much more admirable in his private character than in his public capacity; and the cheerful encouragement he has not unfrequently given to young and diffident beginners, is one proof of an amiable disposition. M

MR. SERGEANT LENS.

A grave aspect, mixt with austerity,
Which should be temper'd so with lenity,
That in them both he might be understood
A scourge to th' ill, a cheerer to the good.
R. Brathwayte's Time's Anatomy.

THE pains taken in a previous article to shew what was meant by the word *gentlemanly,* as applied to the Court of Chancery, will render it less necessary to explain what is to be understood by the word *ungentlemanly,* as applied to the Court of Common Pleas: as in the first it is not to be supposed, that all freedom of speech, or even severity of remark, is banished : so in the last, though there certainly prevails a coarseness of manner, and now and then a vulgarity of expression, it would be an error to say that the restraint

M 2

which well educated men in other situations impose upon themselves are disregarded. Undoubtedly from several causes, to which reference was made in the strictures upon Mr. Sergeant Best, the advocates in the Common Pleas assume and are allowed a far greater degree of licence than is granted in the other Courts: their speeches are frequently more violent, and their examination of witnesses are sometimes conducted with an excess of inconsiderateness, and even fierceness, without a parallel. It would however be extremely unfair to include all the sergeants in this sweeping accusation, and it would be least of all just to the individual who is the subject of the present article; for a man of greater mildness of manner and general propriety of deportment, was perhaps never known than Mr. Sergeant LENS. I never heard of an instance in which he had thrown off his natural suavity, however great might have been the designed provocation: Mr. Sergeant Shepherd has already been excepted, and the same distinction is due to Mr. Sergeant Copley, but not so much on account of his education or the peculiar gentlemanliness of his feelings, as the calculating coldness of his temperament. It is not however to be understood for a moment that Mr. Sergeant LENS wants either resolution or firmness ; on the contrary, his undeviating self-possession is always sure to shew him the clear difference between right and wrong, which some in their passion confound; and when once he is convinced of the solidity of the ground on which he has taken his stand, nothing can shake him—nothing induce him to resign it.

It may seem extraordinary, that with such an example before them, the Advocates should not more have profited by it; but as was said many years ago, " the leaven of ill is alway more powerful than the leaven of good," and it is aided by the cautious reluctance of the judges of the Common Pleas to interpose besides, if Mr. Sergeant LENS be an example of undeviatingly decorous demeanour, Mr Sergeant Vaughan is too often an example of the contrary. As I shall not be able to devote a separate article to him, and as the examination of his character and attainments will be of some use, I shall take this opportunity of summing him up in a few sentences : they are the more fit for this place, because he will be more directly contrasted with the gentleman whose name is placed at the head of the present criticism.

It is but fair to begin with his merits ; and the most prominent and useful of these are great quickness of perception, and uncommon readiness in emergencies ; the next is industry, and the third an apparently deep interest in the event of the cause. It is astonishing sometimes to see of what use the latter is to him : his external anxiety, his unwillingness to give up a point most clearly against him, often has made a jury hesitate about a question on which they would not otherwise have entertained a moment's doubt : it is aided also by an unblushing confidence which, to use a vulgar phrase, sticks at nothing, and which is most shewn when most needed, viz. when his case is good for nothing. He is a tolerably fluent speaker, not because he has a wide

command of language, but because he never
cares what words he employs, and those
which are uppermost and first present themselves are generally the coarsest and most
vulgar; such as many other men would not,
without reluctance, and could not, without
difficulty, have selected. It is obvious that
he has had little or no education, with the
pretence of classical attainments, for he is
very fond of interlarding his addresses with
common-place scraps of Latin, and if without a false quantity, he is more indebted to
his good luck than to his knowledge. I apprehend that he has a very slender stock of
legal information, and he wants the prudence
of which men of mere quickness are often
destitute, to conceal his ignorance. From
what has been said, it will perhaps be inferred, that he is by no means a bad *nisi
prius* advocate in such cases as regard the
warranty and soundness of horses or paltry
assaults; but to weightier matters his strength
is not equal: he is reckoned by some (and
among others perhaps by himself) a man of
considerable wit, and it must be admitted

that he has a share of low humour, which with low people passes for metal of a higher value. I once or twice have heard him open a case where it was impossible to avoid something like the phrazeology of an orator. Perhaps his complete failures on these occasions may prejudice people too much against his efforts in a different stile. I am willing to acknowledge that this may be the case with myself.— *Solum est oratoris dicere, loqui autem communis vulgi.*

Such is Mr. Sergeant Vaughan, whose talents, such as they are, have obtained him a considerable proportion of the business in the Court where he practises : there are few men who form so strong a contrast to him as Mr. Sergeant Lens, who holds quite as many briefs, but, as may be guessed, in causes involving very different questions and interests : his business is not only more respectable but more lucrative. At first sight it would not be supposed that he had the same velocity at catching a point as Mr. Sergeant Vaughan : his countenance does not express it, and per-

haps he has it not in the same degree : his
face, if it be a little marked by grave lines,
is far from having a harsh expression, or can
only be thought so by those who cannot distinguish between the staidness of reflection
and the crabbedness of severity. When
Sir V. Gibbs was on the Bench, and Mr.
Sergeant LENS at Bar, a fine opportunity
was afforded of remarking the difference. Mr.
Sergeant LENS looks as if he were intended
for a judge, and probably the only reason
he is not so, is, that he values so highly the
principles which he first adopted with caution and afterwards adhered to with firmness,
that he would not accept any office which
would bear even the appearance of an abandonment of them.*   Notwithstanding the

It is not my practice to deal in private anecdotes ; or
the contrary I have expressly avoided them, but the fol
lowing reflects so much credit upon the subject of thi
article, and has been so publicly stated, and still remain
uncontradicted, that it cannot be supposed that I am
guilty of any thing like prying into secret history, o
committing a breach of confidence. When the Solicitor
Generalship was vacant about two years ago, it was offere
to Mr. Sergeant LENS, who of course refused it, alledg
ing that the acceptance would be inconsistent with th

number of instances in which he has been
opposed as an advocate to the empty flippancies of Mr. Sergeant Vaughan, and to the
peevish impetuosity of Mr. Sergeant Best,
I am not aware, as I remarked in the outset,
that on any occasion his equanimity has been
disturbed: much may be attributed to the
goodness of his temper, and to the coolness
of his judgment, but perhaps not a little to
the respect which his appearance and demeanour cannot fail to excite: it strikes one
as a thing impossible to offer an offence to
such a man: a generous or a mean spirit
would be afraid to do it; the one because he
would despise himself, the other because he
would be despised.

I do not place him upon a level with mere

political opinions he had always entertained.   Ministers
were in want of his services, well knowing their value,
and proposed, that if he would give them his legal advice,
they would not require that he should sit, speak, or vote
in Parliament.   Mr. Sergeant LENS still adhered to his
first determination, refusing thus to compromise his
principles, and declaring that he would not accept the
place of Solicitor-General at all, if he could not consci-
entiously do so on the same terms as his predecessors.

nisi prius Advocates: it is scarcely fair to
institute a comparison between them, for
there are few persons more distinct than an
able lawyer before a court, and an able counsel before a jury; independent of the different
sort of talent required in the one place and
in the other, the knowledge which is necessary for each is also different: but when I
say that Mr. Sergeant LENS is no match for
some, who consider themselves his rivals, in
the low chicanery and artifices of practice,
his inferiority does not arise from his ignorance of those tricks, but from his contempt
and disdain of them: he will not condescend
to employ them, nor will he ever give them
his support when resorted to by others who
may be coupled with him in the management
of the cause. It should seem as if he had
unluckily fallen upon evil times; as if his
learning, his abilities, and his disposition
were intended for an age, when the petty and
despicable contrivances by which the great
ends of justice are now delayed or defeated,
had either not been invented or were perpe-
tually abolished: he may truly say at the

present moment, and in the present state of
he practice of our Courts,

> This study fits a mercenary drudge
> Who aims at nothing but external trash—
> Too servile and illiberal for me—
>
> *C. Marlow's Faustus*

The mildness and urbanity of deportment,
of which I have already spoken, belongs to
him in all situations, and towards all persons:
how often have the most respectable Solicitors,
who mix in the best companies, and are there
treated as they deserve with the utmost attention, reason to complain of the presumptuous
pettishness of some upstart Barrister who has
attained such a station in his profession as to
command a certain quantity of business.   Sir
W. Garrow was sometimes positively fero-
cious to them if they happened to interrupt
him by any suggestion which did not meet
with his concurrence, and I once saw Sir V.
Gibbs inflict upon an Attorney a very sound
box on the ear in open Court: the man shewed
however that it was in some degree merited
by his patient submission under it. *Aspe-
rius nihil est humili cum surgit in altum* is

an old, but not perhaps a very elegant Latin proverb, which may be applied to many successful Advocates, but never to Mr. Sergeant LENS, who behaves with equal respect towards his inferiors, his equals, and his superiors.

It remains now only for me to say a few words regarding the stile and manner of the individual before us; his mode of speaking is forcible, but its principle fault is that it is too constantly so ; that it has not sufficient variety, that there is too little relief, and that his endeavour to secure attention, and to keep it up as he proceeds now and then defeats itself : his voice too is rather monotonous and heavy in its sound, which tends to increase the defect. His language is always well chosen, and shews that he is a scholar and a man of general education : a vulgarism seldom or never escapes his lips, unless to answer some particular purpose, and his sentences are usually full and complete : they are perhaps somewhat too long and might be advantageously lightened by an occasional interrogation or interjection. On these accounts

N

his stile is much better adapted to a continued
legal argument, than to an address to a jury.
His action has little about it that is remarkable, but certainly nothing that is offensive.
If his style has not much that is fascinating,
it is often most impressive.

Of his learning, I believe, no person competent to form an opinion entertains a doubt;
—his talents, his acquirements, his character,
and his temper, all unite to recommend him
to one of the highest stations of the law:
he has several times presided on the home
circuit when Lord Ellenborough was absent
from illness; and there are I believe few
members of the profession who do not hope
at some distant period to see him confirmed
in the seat which hitherto he has only tem-
porarily occupied.*

* This hope has been for the present at least disappointed. I willingly admit the talents of the present
Lord Chief Justice, nor will he, I am sure, think it any
disparagement to say, that they are inferior to those of
Mr. Sergeant LENS.

MR. DAUNCEY.

False dice will run as smooth as truest bones ;
Fine filed tongues deceive plain people oft ;
Fondlings may take pure glass for precious stones.
T. Churchyard's Honour of the Law. 1596

PERSONS who have not been in the habit of attending the circuits would be astonished to see what very different figures some men cut in town and in the country. A young barrister (by which I mean a man of perhaps from ten to fifteen years standing, but whose name, like Serjeant Eitherside's antagonist, was scarcely known in Westminster-Hall) who has hardly had the opportunity of hearing the sound of his own voice in the metropolis, may enjoy a tolerable share of practice at a distance from it, in the district where his relatives and friends can exert their influence in his favour. This, as I have elsewhere pointed out, is one of the modern modes by which men creep into business: formerly, as many examples would establish, a man of real talents having made a dash in some great case, afterwards commanded employment; but of late years not a single instance of the kind has been known; but individuals have slowly worked their way upwards, first by holding briefs as juniors to a silk gown or a coif, and subsequently by inducing an attorney, with whom they are connected, or with whom they have scraped acquaintance, to entrust them with a leading brief, which gives them a chance of making a speech to a jury: of course they employ the occasion to the best advantage, as far as their talents go—they do their utmost for their client, and independent of the great pains taken, there is something animating, not to say inspiring, in an audience composed of the first gentry of the surrounding counties, and among them, what operates above all upon a young and ardent spirit, not a few females, who, "drest with the lovely time of year," have travelled

far to witness the administration of justice
In London, nearly the whole area of the Cour
is filled by cold-blooded Solicitors, their ig
norant Clerks, and Barristers much more in
clined enviously to detract and discourage
than generously to acknowledge excellenc
and to aid diffident infirmity,—" who sicker
even if a friend prevail," and smile and
chuckle at every new failure.

There are other reasons, besides, quite a
important, why as a general proposition i
may be said, that on the circuits bette
speeches are delivered, and a nearer approacl
made to what may deserve the name of elo
quence, than in London. There seems some
thing damp and depressing in the very air c
Westminster - Hall : we associate with th
thought of it a recollection of the petty state
liness of four men in scarlet or purple, whe
have just stiffness enough to be chilling, with
out dignity enough to be awful : who, nomi
nally presiding in the noblest apartment i
Europe, are in fact boxed up in an insig
nificant corner, as if their intellects were onl

fitted to that contracted sphere; where the deficiency of splendour is attempted to be supplied by a paltry tapestry of the royal arms, and the absence of true majesty by the wooden representatives of four kings with gilt globes, sceptres, and crowns. In some of the fine town-halls in the country, at least much of this is got rid of: the business, too, is usually placed in a greater variety of hands; we have not the perpetual and wearisome recurrence of the same counsel with the same peculiarities and habits in every cause, but, as I have said, more room is given for rising ambition, and for the talent by which it is most frequently accompanied. Let me add too, that a Judge at the assizes is a personage of much greater apparent consequence than elsewhere—he is surrounded by a great deal more pomp and circumstance—trumpeters for state, and javelin-men for guard—and, to use rather a vulgarism, he is therefore somewhat more upon his good behaviour, particularly in Court, where he generally makes all possible efforts to keep up his artificial consequence: for this reason, perhaps, his

temper is not so easily ruffled, and he endea
vours as much to controul himself as othen
Counsel on this account, and on others tha
could be easily enumerated if necessary, ai
not so frequently interrupted by the Bench
a greater degree of latitude is allowed, an
greater indulgence is shewn to those who ma
have been less accustomed, if not less incline
to submit. Though Lawyers, educated in
contempt for every thing but their own im
mediate pursuit, (which if they did not fei
they would entertain perhaps a thorough con
tempt for themselves) are of all men the leas
sensible of the beautiful in nature, and thoug
most of them, when travelling from town t
town, are much more intent upon the pros
pect of their fees than of the country, yet a
cannot be alike dead in this respect ; it woul
perhaps be too much to say, that even th
dullest and most calculating was not in som
degree or other operated upon and improve
by beholding the contrast to "the smoke an
stir of this dim spot,"—London. One o
our first legal orators was once asked b
a poring plodder of Pump Court, how h

managed to make such good speeches, and
the often-quoted reply was, " Sir, my Cham-
bers look upon the Thames." That the answer was unintelligible to the questioner ,we
may easily believe—he had never heard of
Sir John Denham's celebrated lines, and probably, had not the remotest notion that there
was any thing in the view of a majestic river
that could even more easily afford " a great
example" to an orator than to a poet.

Yet, if leading brief on the circuits now
and then fall into young hands, those who
hold them are apt to fall into young errors:
the patience shewn by the Judges of assize
sometimes occasions a needless waste of time,
by the enforcing of points of little consequence, or by miscalculated exertions to asto-
nish: a young speaker of promise will be
almost sure, at first, to deviate into bombast
or balderdash; yet this is scarcely to be called
a fault, when compared with the cropped
and clipped business-like speeches of Counsel in London: it is only the exuberance and
extravagance of that, which, if pruned by

good taste, instead of being usually cut ι
by the roots by merciless caprice and il
temper, would bear not only the blosson
but the fruits of eloquence—I do not sa
that this exuberance prevails to any conside
able extent—certainly not—I wish it did
but the reverse of wrong is not always righ
and this has no doubt led a younker or tw
to bring eloquence into disrepute, by imagii
ing that to make a fine speech little more wi
necessary than to do exactly the contrary (
what he had seen performed by many of tl
older stagers in Westminster-Hall. The in
dulgence too of country audiences, or th
bad taste and bad judgment of the approvin
friends of these would-be orators, preveni
them from seeing their errors, and their blind
ness is aided by the want of more living ex
amples of excellence in this kind.

These remarks have been partly produce
by reflecting upon the great popularity ac
quired by Mr. DAUNCEY on the Oxfor
circuit, while his talents, such as they are, ar
comparatively but little known and esteemer

in London. This circumstance is to be attributed in some degree to the fact, that here he confines his practice exclusively to the Exchequer, the proceedings in which are seldom noticed in the newspapers, (the usual channels of legal information,) and to which persons seldom resort as parties but upon compulsion, when informations for a breech of some of the revenue laws are filed against them.   Although it is a Court of Equity as well as of Law, what is done in the former is even less known than in the latter.

Perhaps I ought to speak with some diffi-dence as to the talents and qualifications of the subject of this article, because I readily confess that I have not had the same means of forming a judgment as I have possessed with regard to some other men ; but I have seen him engaged in important causes in the country not once nor twice ; and it always struck me, that he by no means deserved the reputation he has acquired.   It has often been remarked, that there are some men who never grow wiser from the contemplation of their

own faults, because they cannot see them
they may be perfectly alive to the errors o
others, but they have the ordinary huma
infirmity of not being alive to their own ;—
so it is, I apprehend, with Mr. DAUNCEY
for the greatest mistakes he commits—th
blunders into which he now and then ur
happily falls, arise from not knowing himself
from not being aware to what he is compe
tent and what is infinitely beyond his reacl
Owing to this weakness he sometimes " prove
himself a fool in what he would fain seer
most wise ;" and this false estimate has le
to injurious consequences, not merely to hin
self, but to his clients. For instance, nobod
can doubt, who has only heard him once o
twice, that he thinks himself a very goo
speech-maker, not to say orator, and c
this account he avails himself at the assiz
of every opportunity of making a display o
what he conceives a peculiar talent; " I
will talk you for an hour on the end of
straw," like a man who professes to walk a
hundred miles on a cabbage leaf, and imagin
all the time that he is exceedingly entertaii

ing, and is making a rapid progress toward
the end of a cause, which he is sure to persuad
himself must terminate in his favour: whe
however the verdict is given against him, h
appears astonished at the summing up of th
Judge, who did not see things exactly in th
light in which he had viewed them, and a
the stupidity and perverseness of the Jury
that did not pay more attention and deferenc
to his address than to the real merits. I
fact, I consider Mr. DAUNCEY little mor
than a mere talker, who after long practic
has attained a great facility in stringing sentences together; and it would be singula
indeed if among so many he did not now and
then " stumble on a virtue unawares," and
say something that was tolerable. Swift's
celebrated Laputan machine for mixing and
jumbling all sorts of words, was sometimes
effectual in producing a line or two that
looked like connected poetry. If then it b
asked, how he has obtained the character and
the business he enjoys, I answer, by having
and having had no rivals—that is to say, no
persons who could address a jury as well as

well as himself, however ill in the estimation of some that may be. The Oxford circuit may be considered remarkable for advocates who can talk and who cannot talk : Mr. DAUNCEY can talk a great deal—Mr. Jervis not a little, and Mr. Campbell and Mr. Puller not at all :* Mr. Taunton, who accompanies them, pretends to little more than being a lawyer ; so that Mr. DAUNCEY, has no adequate antagonist; for Mr. Jervis, who has also a silk gown, and is a most amiable man, cannot cope with his volubility, which in the country is easily mistaken for something much better. The current of a paltry mill-stream is often much more rapid and noisy than the tide of a large river.

---

* When I say " not at all," I wish to be understood in a qualified sense. Of course both these latter gentle men have words enough, but they have very seldom " fit words in fit places." They are both of them tole rably quick, particularly the latter, while the forme has devoted much labour and study to his profession Mr. Campbell is not so hesitating as inefficient ; i speaking he keeps his finger tediously elevated near th side of his head. Mr. Puller has a short snappish mod of delivery, quite as unimpressive, but varied and re lieved now and then by a few disconcerted pauses.

O

What has contributed to that which I feel inclined to call the deception, is a certain portion of quickness and cunning, which is no doubt possessed by the individual in question, and which many unreflecting and inexperienced people reckon qualifications of great rarity and of the highest excellence. The first, however, belongs to every clever schoolboy; and the last, when it amounts to nothing more than mere cunning, of itself proves the absence of nobler requisites : cunning, as applied to a barrister, is generally an endeavour to supply the place of and to make up for other deficiencies. At the same time it is often useful in detecting falsehood, where a witness is a fool; but cunning is easily met by cunning, and a witness is frequently an over-match for an advocate who has no other resources : *in laqueos quos posuit cadit.* Mr. DAUNCEY has a good deal of artifice, but he has always wanted commanding power : he never

---

————————————in his hand the iron flail did hold,
With which he thrash'd out falsehood, and did truth
unfold ;

but his contrivances are too frequently petty and insignificant, and of course what he accomplishes bears its proportion to the means employed.

Of the furniture of his mind I can say but little; it certainly does not appear to possess any great solidity—rather for ornament than for use: were he master of any considerable resources, I think he has cleverness enough to bring them forward; but they have never made their appearance when I had an opportunity of hearing him. I am told that he has a humourous way of relating a story out of *Joe Miller* or some other jest book, and this would go a great way in the provinces to persuade the uneducated inhabitants that he must be a man of very superior abilities.

" Though a dram of sweet be worth a pound of sour," after what I have said in dispraise of MR. DAUNCEY, it will perhaps not be easy to satisfy his numerous and partial friends by any applause I can bestow upon his appearance and manner : both, but especially the last, are much in his favour: his countenance is vivid and expressive—his voice clear and tolerably harmonious, though nasal; and his action generally easy and appropriate. I know no man at present at the bar who excels him in the use of his arms; yet, like most persons in the habit of speaking at a table, he is too apt to visit it with severe inflictions. In externals, he leaves little to be desired.*

* The subject of the above article has died during its progress through the press, the second time. The author did not think it necessary to withdraw it from the original collection.

MR. GURNEY.

It is my way to consider men as they stand in merit, no
according to their fortune or figure.—*Tatler*, No. 34.

THE observation is considerably older than
the time of Mandeville, author of the *Fable of
the Bees*, that talents and attainments rather
below than above mediocrity, are much more
useful to a man, who wishes to thrive and
grow rich in society, than abilities and knowledge of the highest order: this is less para-
doxical, and consequently more intelligible
at first sight, than many other positions in
that most clever of all clever books, where we
are in every page startled by apparent absurdities and contradictions so ingeniously re-
conciled, that whereas in the outset we laugh-
ed at the author, in the end we pity ourselves
The remark above quoted is true in every si-

o 3

tuation of life.   Genius is a most unsaleable
commodity, while mediocrity is the real phi-
losopher's stone.   Looking round among our
connexions and acquaintances, we shall be
sure to find those best off in the world, not
who have the most, but who have the least
genius, and who, perhaps, without quickness
enough to be aware of the deficiency, uncon-
sciously make up for it in some other way,
being gifted with qualities of a much more
profitable kind : if they are dull, they are
the more fit for drudges; and as society is at
present constituted, much more is to be accomplished by patient perseverance in old
courses, than by any of the highest and luck-
est hits of inventive talent.   Steele observes,
' that it is the misfortune of persons of great
genius to have their faculties dissipated by
attention to too many things at once ;" they
are " every thing by fits and nothing long ;"
they are the schemers and projectors of the
world, who put forth plans of improvement,
which are ridiculed, but which when carried
into execution by mechanical industry, become the delight and glory of mankind.

Of course the pursuits of commerce call into action but few of the better qualities of our nature : men of genius will seldom condescend to engage their faculties in low barter and petty traffic ; but some portion of talent is necessary, and we can most of us recollect instances of merchants and tradesmen, who, having gradually acquired wealth, afterwards retired into the country to enjoy their gains, as far as such men are capable of such enjoyments: yet it will almost invariably be found, that those who have the finest country houses and the gayest equipages, are those who have shewn even less talent and possess less general information than their rivals in trade. The same may be said of the arts: in painting, for example, a man who can produce smooth flattering portraits, but just resembling the originals, and so like each other as to be destitute of all distinguishing character, is knighted by Princes, visited by nobles, *cheri des grands, aimé des belles*, and dispatched to a Congress of assembled Potentates ; while a historical painter, who deals with the imagination as well as the mechanism of his art,

an neither find purchasers for his pictures,
nor patronage for himself.   It applies no less
to what are called the liberal professions.
Divines who fatten upon lucrative livings
(not referring here to honours but to emoluments) are the " round oily men of God,"
who, with very moderate gifts of intellect,
slide into the good things of this world, never
presenting any points of opposition.   Physicians of abilities and enterprise above the
ordinary level, incur the charge of being
quacksalvers and empirics, while those who
only plod in the steps of their predecessors,
without attempting any improvement in a
science so obviously in its infancy, are esteemed most sagacious and infallible.

Although in the law it has more frequently
happened, from various causes to which on
former occasions reference has been made, that
men of first-rate abilities have forced their
way forward in spite of all the resistance of
prejudice and envy, and have now and then
secured ample fortunes, yet even here mediocrity has its advantages, and those exclusive,

peculiar, and of no slight importance. For instance, a Barrister who has plain good sense enough to know that he has not commanding talents, such as will compel the Court to listen to him with patience, and Attornies to give him briefs, will make himself master of all the arts of conciliation; will never attempt to resist the declared opinion of their Lordships, however absurd it may appear, but will patiently submit to whatever they shall dictate: the ear of the Court having been thus obtained, it is soon known who is the favourite Counsel, and without any considerable display on his part of the ingenious art of *hugging*, (though never backward to shew his skill in that way) business will flow into his hands almost unsought for. It is too obvious to need proof, that a man of true genius will never condescend to such low practices and artifices, and if he succeed, as I have said, it is in despite of obstacles which other men have neither the courage to meet nor the talent to surmount.— In the same way, a man of mediocre ability prudently adopts all means to countervail his defects: he supplies the place of eloquence by diligence: he reads his instructions with

rity.   He is c
the ablest Cha
great seal, an
as an opinion
seems *to be a*
is well instruc
fession.   He
the oldest and
suitors who ar
advocates are
unheard.   H
declared that
to devote his
such a predic
needlessly int
pelled them
tality, was u
him. * *This*
this gentlema
played by Lc
years, withou

* In the case
Lord Eldon's re
address to His Lc
of two days, and

peculiar, and of no slight importance. For instance, a Barrister who has plain good sense enough to know that he has not commanding talents, such as will compel the Court to listen to him with patience, and Attornies to give him briefs, will make himself master of all the arts of conciliation; will never attempt to resist the declared opinion of their Lordships, however absurd it may appear, but will patiently submit to whatever they shall dictate: the ear of the Court having been thus obtained, it is soon known who is the favourite Counsel, and without any considerable display on his part of the ingenious art of *hugging*, (though never backward to shew his skill in that way) business will flow into his hands almost unsought for. It is too obvious to need proof, that a man of true genius will never condescend to such low practices and artifices, and if he succeed, as I have said, it is in despite of obstacles which other men have neither the courage to meet nor the talent to surmount.—In the same way, a man of mediocre ability prudently adopts all means to countervail his defects: he supplies the place of eloquence by diligence: he reads his instructions with

great attention and industry, and by prudence
and waryness, endeavours to divert, if he cannot combat, the attacks of his antagonists.

I know that there are many persons in
London, and in the country too, as far as the
home circuit extends, who consider Mr. GUR-
NEY a Counsel of first rate talents: I am not
one of his unqualified admirers; and though
I think him a good advocate, I am very far
from being of opinion that he deserves the
epithet of an able one. Circumstances have
greatly contributed to bring him forward, or
he would probably still have continued behind the Bar, from whence he was taken only
about two years ago: were it otherwise, we
might be at a loss to account for the change
that has so rapidly taken place in public opinion regarding him: those who are only
young in their recollections of these matters
know that very few years are past since Mr.
GURNEY thought himself fortunate if he made
but a small profit beyond the expences of his
circuit. He was made King's Counsel at a
most fortunate time, when Sir W. Garrow
either had retired or was about to retire, and

when the ill-health of Mr. Topping, independent of his defects and deficiencies, had rendered him altogether incapable of competing with Mr. Scarlett. At this period, Mr. GURNEY, who had often made himself useful in government prosecutions of all kinds, came forward, and as it was known that he had the ear of the Court, and that Mr. Marryat (who obtained a silk gown at the same date) had not, he immediately obtained a considerable share of business, principally as the rival of Mr. Scarlett: when the latter was secured on one side of a cause, Mr. GURNEY was most commonly retained on the other. Yet they were by no means equally matched in any respect, Mr. Scarlett certainly being a man of very eminent talents and attainments, and Mr. GURNEY's principal recommendation being that mediocrity, and some of its useful concomitants, of which I have before spoken. Among those concomitants is that conciliatory temper, which is not easily ruffled, and which seems to take all possible pains to make friends : he has the good sense to perceive in the words of Pascal, that *les hommes se gouvernent plus par caprices qu ar raison*, and he is very careful to accommodate himself to them : at least he used to be so, though I have some reason to think that he at present presumes a little upon his rank and the quantity of business he had obtained, though he still preserves that respectful demeanour towards the Court which has contributed to establish him so firmly in its favour. No man will deny that great deference ought to be shewn even to an intimation from the Bench, but it may be, and often is, carried to such an excess as materially to interfere with the due administration of justice. For the same reason that he is conciliatory, Mr. GURNEY is patient and industrious to the last degree: he spares no trouble in reading and noting all the particulars communicated by those from whom he receives his instructions ; and when he is called upon to address a Jury he usually provides himself with the principal topics, cut and dried, and registered in short-hand, on one of the blank leaves of his brief. He has besides the advantage of being a very expert short-hand writer, which gives him the appearance, to those who are not aware of the facility, of being not only a

more accurate, but a quicker man than some
of his opponents.

In one respect, let me do the subject of this
article the justice to observe, that he exceeds
most of those with whom he has to contend.
I mean the extreme prudence that he invariably displays in the conduct of a cause : as
he makes himself well acquainted with the
facts, and the nature of the evidence to support them, he is seldom taken by surprise :
this remark applies to his own case only ;
but in attacking that of his adversary his
caution and wariness are sometimes in his
way ; he is too much afraid of committing
himself and his client, and he therefore leaves
undone what it is obvious to every one else
might be accomplished, had he courage to
make the attempt : thus it by no means unfrequently happens, that a fraudulent and
designing witness escapes detection, unless the
Attorney has been able previously to sift out
some suspicious circumstances, and to communicate them to the Counsel, which warrant
him in putting questions which he would other-

P

wise never have hazarded. The faculty of
looking through a witness at a glance, and of
letting him know that you look through him,
is certainly a gift which may be improved by
habit; but I do not think that Mr. GURNEY
ever possessed this important qualification of
an Advocate even in a slight degree; and
perhaps from a knowledge of this deficiency
has arisen the extreme and sometimes injurious caution of which I have spoken. Were
not this intuitive faculty a gift and not merely
an acquisition, it is not very easy to account
for the total absence of it in Mr. GURNEY, as
from his long practice at the Sessions and at
the Old Bailey, among the most depraved of
mankind, he would otherwise have attained it
to some perfection. On this account, it will
be concluded that he is by no means a good
examiner of a witness excepting in one respect; that his great care leads him often to
put a question very ingeniously, and to wind
round and to beat about a point with considerable skill, because he trembles for the consequences of coming to it at once. There are
however few men who have a better mode of

making a witness tell a long, complicated story, full of minute details, with regularity and clearness.

As a speaker he possesses but little that is remarkable, excepting a facility (in part mechanical from the rapidity with which he writes short-hand, and thus puts all the main facts before his eyes at one view) of giving a Jury a distinct knowledge of the case he has to bring forward in evidence; he arranges all the particulars historically, and is always extremely accurate as to dates. At the same time I ought to allow, I have sometimes heard him forcible, if not eloquent, and if his general observations be not of a very novel character the gravity and sagaciousness of his look frequently imposes a common-place upon his audience with much of the effect of originality. This observation, and indeed all I have said about his mode of speaking, cannot be illustrated better, than by a reference to his celebrated address on bringing the horrid case of *Chalcraft and Chennell* before a Jury at late Surry Assizes: all his introductory re

P 2

narks were as trite as he could well make
hem, but his detail of the facts was perspicu-
us and convincing.

Mr. GURNEY is considered in the professi-
n a tolerable criminal Lawyer, but nothing
1ore : he certainly never affects to be learned
ither in principles or precedents; and when-
ver, in the course of a cause at *Nisi Prius*, a
 oint arises, he always endeavours to avoid it,
nd to throw the weight of the argument up-
n the shoulders of his junior : in this respect
 e forms a contrast to Mr. Scarlett, who ne-
er shrinks on such an occasion, but seems to
 ke pleasure in grappling with and overcom-
1g the difficulty.   As to the general informa-
ion of the individual whose qualifications are
nder discussion, I do not feel myself very
ompetent to speak : all I can say is, that if
 e seldom betrays ignorance, he never dis-
 lays knowledge; and I apprehend that his
 fe has been too actively employed to enable
 im to acquire much beyond what he may
 ave learnt from the conversation of those by
 hom he is surrounded.

MR. DENMAN.

A visage sterne and milde, where both did growe
Vice to contemne, in vertue to rejoice :
Amid great stormes whom grace assured so
To live upright and smile at Fortune's choyce.

Lord Surrey's Poems.

THERE is this to be said of preeminent ability, that it is the object of envy with no man ; emulation, an honest struggle to deserve by doing as well, it will, and ought to, excite : but the aim of envy is lower, it looks only to the end ; it does not care for the means but the accomplishment ; and provided it can perform as much and acquire as much with talents far inferior, it has attained its purpose and is contented. "Envy is a vile passion——it has its birth in base minds ;" and as those who are afflicted with it are incapa-

P 3

ble of understanding and estimating what is really great, they are incapable of envying it: a man may envy a painter the emoluments of his pencil, but not the talent that guides it—he may envy a poet the price of his productions, not the genius that dictated them—he may envy an eloquent advocate the amount of his fees, but if by tricks and imposition he can obtain as large a share of business, he will turn learning and eloquence into ridicule, and hug himself that he can with impunity commit such easy and successful frauds.

There is probably no profession where so much encouragement is given to envy as in the law: the love of gain there is the principally operating motive, for even the gratification of ambition is generally made subservient to it, and a barrister will very commonly, when offered a situation of judicial eminence, (though he may already have acquired a large fortune,) strike a balance of profit and loss, and refuse the intended honours, because his emoluments would be

reduced by acceptance. The means too by
which wealth is acquired among these *fruges*
consumere natos are chiefly such as may be
subject to envy, particularly of late, since
the comparative degradation of the Bar, and
the absence or banishment of what was formerly understood by the term eloquence:
I use the term banishment because I feel satisfied that it is only excluded by the degenerate
nature of modern practice, and that were due
encouragement given, were our judges less
men of forms and more men of liberal attainments, it might, even in the course of a few
years, be restored. Notwithstanding all the
exertions of that " pompous piece of puff
paste," Mr. Phillips, to bring the Irish Bar
into discredit with people of taste and under
standing, we cannot entertain a doubt that
the counsel in the courts of the sister-king
dom are far better speech-makers than those
on this side of the channel ; and the reason i
connected with various points to which
adverted in my first article, where I mentioned
some of the causes of the decline of the English
Bar. On this account, too, if I may rely on

information I have received, there prevails among the barristers in Dublin much more friendship and cordiality than among those in London: there is less room for the display of trickery and cunning by which, with us, so much money is made, and the possession and employment of real eloquence and talents is, as I have said above, the low mark at which envy levels. The difference is perceptible even in the very commencement of the pursuit, for making all due allowances for the more sociable and convivial spirit of our neighbours, (which social and convivial spirit, by the bye, is engendered and fostered by the absence of this base passion,) let any man observe the difference in the behaviour of the English and Irish students when dining in the hall of the Middle Temple : so strong is the contrast, that it has led to the separation of the one from the other, and the sides of the apartment are called according to the natives of the different countries which usually occupy them. I am no admirer of the flippant flourishes of the sons of St. Patrick, nor of their unrestrained self-confidence, but I am an admirer of the warmth of feeling and generosity óf disposition they seem to possess. No doubt those who sit on the English side of the Hall are much harder readers, but they confound and bewilder their understandings, and one would have thought that they could have spared a single hour of the day cheerfully to shake hands and discuss the current topics of conversation. But no; generally a dead silence prevails, and men sit opposite to each other as if they sat opposite a dead wall, or automatons at best, and seem to have little in common but the dish out of which they carve, and the dulness which the countenance of the one seems to reflect from the visage of the other. This however is not invariably the case; two or three pupils of the same pleader or barrister sometimes join in a mess, (for so each division of four students is termed) and by the help of discussions upon pleas, rejoinders and demurrers, drawn or considered in the course of the morning, a conversation is kept going, if it cannot be said to be kept alive: if however a fourth person, a stranger, happen by chance and of necessity to sit with them, if he be not looked upon quite as an intruder, he is excluded from almost every thing but what is connected with mere eating and drinking.

If in Court the barristers are more communicative among each other, it is rather by compulsion than by choice: it is a matter of business to attend, during term at least, and wearied with hearing the same thing over and over again, they now and then talk in self-defence against *ennui,* or the languor arising from thinking little and doing nothing. Yet there seems to be a want of heart in whatever they say—they talk to please themselves not others, and if in conversation one man says a cleverer thing than another, it is of course an offence to the self-love of all his hearers. In this respect, it must be admitted, they are generally very forbearing, and it has astonished not a few to see how possible it is for a number of men of education to sit for hours together without the utterance of one thing deserving recollection. The envious feeling of which I have spoken is encouraged also by the contact into which the parties are brought: they are everlastingly on the watch not to improve themselves by imitating excellence, but to degrade others by exaggerating defects and disseminating failures : if a counsel commit an error, or receive a rebuke from the Bench, it is met by a general titter of congratulation—one proof of the ancient position that laughter arises from a supposed sense of superiority—nor does it end here, for the misfortune is retailed in all companies, as if with an anxious endeavour to spread the intelligence as widely as possible.

Mr. DENMAN is not a man whose attainments or talents are calculated to excite envy, not because they are below it, (for nothing is below it which produces money,) but because they are so eminent, as to be above the understanding of those who are slaves to it: neither are the profits he derives from his professional pursuits, yet such as to excite the general hostility of those who may consider hemselves his rivals. He has however attained considerable business in the Midland Circuit,

where almost his only worthy competitor was
Mr. Serjeant Copley recently made Chief
Justice of Chester.* I have already given
my opinion regarding Mr. Serjeant Vaughan
and his claims to the practice he enjoys, when
I spoke of Mr. Sergeant Lens, and I have
omitted Mr. Clarke purposely, because I do
not think his character possesses any distinguishing features. When I observed above
that Mr. Sergeant Copley was *almost* the only
worthy competitor of Mr. DENMAN on that
circuit, I had in my memory a man of a
well constructed and well informed mind, and
I believe of a most amiable temper and disposition, Mr. Phillipps, author of a book on
Evidence which all competent judges admit
to be a production of first rate excellence in
every way : yet I do not think that he is
equal to Mr. DENMAN, nor will he attain
the same ultimate eminence : his knowledge,
general and particular, is indisputably considerable, but he has important defects to
overcome as an Advocate, and especially a
degree of self-distrust, which he cannot con-

* And now Solicitor-General.

ceal, and which is a very great and dis-
tressing draw-back to a barrister. Mr
DENMAN also has most assuredly the same
defect, but he has more art in not betraying
it; and, when addressing a jury, he can
assume an assured air very opposite from his
nature, but very useful to his success. This
however, is not done at all offensively; it appears the effect of a strong conviction of the
truth of what he is delivering, and not of a
fixed determination and studied endeavour to
impose. His countenance very much aid
him in this particular; it possesses a sedate
gravity, at the same moment both " stern and
mild;" firm without fierceness, and sever
without austerity—thoughtful, penetrating
and serene; indicating a temper not easily
moved, yet not by any means devoid of feel
ing and expression : in short he looks, and a
far as I know any thing of him, is much bette
than a mere lawyer.

But though far from a mere lawyer, I ap
prehend that there are very few men mor
deeply read in the learning of his profession

f I mistake not he was a pupil of one of he most eminent Judges that ever sat upon he King's Bench—I mean Mr. Justice Dampier, who is recorded to have said of the subject of the present article that he was the only student he ever knew, of his own accord, ead Coke upon Littleton, and pursue that branch of the law, strange as it may seem, with a degree of enthusiasm. His practice in Court, and the attentive respect with which he Judges listen to Mr. DENMAN, prove that a very high opinion is entertained of his attainments strictly professional.

Rarely as the varied qualifications are united, Mr. DENMAN is also an excellent *nisi prius* advocate : his delivery is regular and luent, and above all extremely impressive : his voice, I allow, is deep and at times heavy, but it well accords with the sobriety of his whole appearance : he has not, like Mr. Nolan, he person of Stentor and the voice of Bathyllus—there is a harmony in his whole appearance which claims confidence the moment he ises, and before he opens his lips.   His

greatest fault is want of relief, of light and
shade in his speeches: he sometimes wearies
his hearers by his own earnestness, and by
the fixed attention he invariably claims from
them: this too is a defect that I do not think
it probable he will be able to overcome, for,
though a cheerful man, he is far removed
from a joker, and I do not think has a strong
relish for wit or humour. Of course my
knowledge upon this point, as I have seen
him only in public, must be very imperfect.

During the last session Mr. DENMAN sat
in the House of Commons, and uniformly
voted with the Opposition: Mr. Sergeant
Copley, his circuit companion, as uniformly
voted with the Ministers, and the consequence
has been, that the latter is Solicitor-general,
when the former has not even a silk gown.
As a parliamentary speaker I shall hereafter
criticise Mr. Sergeant Copley, and I am
reluctantly compelled to allow that in the
same capacity Mr. DENMAN has by no means
realized my expectations—hitherto I think
he has failed, but let it be remembered that
he only made one speech of length and im-

portance during the session, and that upon the point of granting 10,000*l.* per annum to the Duke of York, as *custos* or keeper to the King. He principally opposed himself to an address made by Mr. Peel, (a young man of over-rated abilities, and who will never do better than he has done, nor attain a higher rank than that of a debater,) and it had the disadvantage of looking like a set speech; for Mr. DENMAN, needlessly distrusting his own powers in a situation to him of some novelty, availed himself of notes, and of this circumstance his artful adversary (who will take the word artful as a compliment) availed himself to charge Mr. DENMAN with a three-days pondered attack. I regretted, too, then to hear Mr. DENMAN make so wide a range over the condition and affairs of the country, when so many fitter opportunities might have been chosen, and which he has subsequently allowed to escape. Notwithstanding this partial disappointment, I am confident, if his professional pursuits do not too much interfere, that he possesses qualifications to render him a very distinguished parliamentary speaker,

MR. SERGEANT COPLEY.[*]

The worth of all men by their end esteem,
And then due praise a due reproach them yield.

Spencer's F. Q. B. II. C. 8.

MANY persons express astonishment, that o
all the practising Lawyers that ever obtained
seats in the House of Commons, so very few
have succeeded as parliamentary orators. I
is here to be understood, that by a parliamentary orator is not meant a mere debater, who
catches at points, and quibbles about words
—who, instead of meeting any great question
of public policy upon enlarged and fair
grounds, confines himself to haggling at particular expressions, and dwelling upon insignificant and uninfluencing trifles.[†] For such

Q 3

[*] Now Solicitor-general; one of the golden fruits of
tergiversation.

[†] Exactly such a man, for instance, was the late Mr.
Perceval, who sometimes thus gained a petty and temporary triumph over his antagonists on the Opposition

a task no man is often better fit than a barrister
who has attained a plausible volubility : but
a parliamentary orator is a being of quite a
different order—whose talents and attainments
are of a totally different class, and are applied
to a different purpose.   The truth however is,
that the English Bar can never be the school
of genuine eloquence : a young man, when he
puts on his paraphernalia, however wide may
be the sphere of his knowledge, and however
enlarged his views, must be content to narrow
his mind and his matter to a small circle :
when he obtains business (if that ever should
happen) it will be impossible for him to employ . and give effect to general principles.
Such an opportunity scarcely occurs in a
century, or if it do occur, he will probably
not be allowed to avail himself of it : the facts
of the particular case, and the little technical
points arising out of them, are all he can look
at : he cannot travel beyond his tether, or out
of the four corners of his record, and must go
over the same ground again and again, with-

side of the House—even over Whitbread,—
    " Whose mighty heart disdain'd to stoop so low,"
as such a push-pin controversy.

out the hope of finding any thing new. A length it becomes habitual; the action of his faculties is limited to so small a compass, that they are at last incapable of wide and general operation; as a man who all his life has been engaged in casting the shuttle, is ultimately rendered incapable of hurling the bar: the strength originally given him is paralized, or rather his elastic muscles are stiffened and contracted. To a certain extent, this is no less true of those Lawyers who do not practise themselves, but are frequent, not to say constant, attendants upon our Courts: they listen to others, and acquire the same modes of thinking, from an unconscious though active principle of imitation. The wonder therefore is not, that Barristers do not succeed, but that they ever have succeeded. If they have attained any eminence in the House of Commons, it has been chiefly by comparison with bad speakers, when men

> Che per se stessi son levati à volo
> Uscendo for de la commune gabbia.
>> *Petr. Tr. del Tempo.*

have disappeared. Of this the state of public speaking in our Parliament at the present day

s one proof out of many others that could be
dduced—Mr. Perceval became, in popular
stimation, an admirable speaker, after Pitt
nd Fox were dead, and Sheridan had retired
rom public life.

Besides the impediment above mentioned,
here is another equally operative, if not
qually important: Counsel, when conduc-
ing a cause at *Nisi Prius* (for before a Jury
. man's real merits are best estimated) think
t necessary to keep their eyes open to all
ides ; not to attend solely to what they find
n their own brief and to what their own wit-
esses will prove, but as far as possible to
nticipate what is to be offered and establish-
d by their antagonists ; the less it is neces-
ary to do so the better, because it is always
onsidered a proof of weakness, if not in the
Jounsel, in the case ; and an excessive cau-
ion in this respect, (as I had reason to ob-
erve before, when noticing Mr. Gurney)
ften occasions defeat : I am persuaded
hat not a few verdicts have been lost by
auseless apprehensions that they might be
ndangered. But if it be necessary in our

Courts, it is surely very seldom required in
our Legislature: the purpose in the one case
is to convince a Jury, often by taking advan
tage of their weaknesses and their prejudices
or in plainer terms, by imposing as much a
possible upon their understandings; but is o
can this be the purpose of a Senator, who is
addressing himself not to any particular set o
men, but to the whole Country; who is no
confining his views to petty facts and point:
concerning the interests of two contending
tradesmen, but applying his intellect and hi
learning to the discusion of a great nationa
question, and to the application of principle
affecting perhaps not merely one state o
community, but the whole civilized world
This is the proper field for genuine eloquence
—this its proper school; here may be displayed and employed all the power and majesty of language—all the comprehensivenes
and vigour of thought—all the fruits independent of the bare facts of learning; all that
wisdom which is the joint produce of reflection, reading, and experience. Here it is,
that the anticipation of objections for the mere

purpose of replying to them is not only use-
ess, but injurious, excepting in some few
special cases : here it is, that all the argu-
nents to enforce and illustrate ought to be
:oncentrated: the opponents ought to be left
o discover their own objections and to sup-
)ort their own arguments: the tide should
)nly set one way : in great rivers, shoals and
]uicksands are produced by the eflux and
eflux of the waters,—by their return and
itoppage,—and in great speeches the weak-
1esses and errors are occasioned by the checks
ind lets given by the orator himself to the
anresisted progress of his eloquence.

One great fault therefore of Lawyers, when
they obtain seats in Parliament and start as
politicians, is, that instead of pressing forward
what makes for their own side of the question
—by urging point after point, and driving
wedge after wedge with increased force (like
the seven progressively sturdy anvil-men in
the 4th Book of the *Fairy Queen :)* instead of
adding new strength and acquiring a fresh
impetus at every step, they pause, and turn

out of their direct course, to answer something which they fancy might be urged against them. This error not unfrequently arises from a sort of apprehension, that if those topics were not adverted to, it would be said that they wanted sagacity or shrewdness to discover the arguments on the other side; from an affectation of quickness of perception and a pretence to foresight, when no man but a fool could suppose, after an orator has made an able address in favour of one position, that he was totally ignorant of the points from which it could be assailed. Of course this rule is general and liable to exceptions, particularly with practised speakers in Parliament: to refute by anticipation is sometimes important, but to a young man, and especially to a young Lawyer, who wishes to attain the character of an orator in the House of Commons, nothing can be more detrimental. It is generally quite enough, for any individual, however powerful his intellect and however extensive his resources, to manage one side of a question; to apply his whole force and energy to that only: his speech will then be much more effective and convincing; as the massive swords formerly employed by our ancestors, requiring the strength of both arms to wield them, were much more destructive than the paltry bodkins with which some of their adversaries furnished either hand, and attempted, first on one side and then on the other, to prick some paltry hole in a part where the armour was least invulnerable.

Mr. Sergeant COPLEY came into Parliament late in the Session before last, after the principal questions regarding the Habeas Corpus Act and other important matters had, I believe, been decided ; but I well recollect one speech made by him upon the Alien Bill, and, if I am not misinformed, he previously offered some observations upou matters almost exclusively legal. Of the first the newspapers gave but a very imperfect account, and of the last they said nothing at all; but I was fortunately present when the debate upon the Alien Bill took place, so that, making due allowances for a maiden speech, I could form some estimate of the sort of stile of address Mr.

Sergeant COPLEY would adopt, or more properly speaking, pursue; for he carried into the House of Commons precisely the manner almost peculiar to our Courts of Justice.

It is well known that he was educated, commenced his career, and ran a considerable part of his course, as a Whig, and that, like many of those who differ from their antagonists chiefly in being *out* instead of *in*, he has thought fit of late, in consideration, as it is said, of certain invitations and promises, to change his party if not his politics. I refer to this circumstance not as any thing extraordinary, nor to draw down upon him the enmity of those with whom he formerly professed to think and certainly acted; but merely for the purpose of remarking, that the plan he has pursued in this respect is such as might be expected from his well-known prudence and sagacity. Every ambitionist, whose sole object is political advancement, without regard to the means, must know that the surest mode is to begin in opposition to those whom he intends to join as soon as a fair opportunity

R

is afforded : if a pamphleteer wishes for a bribe, he must be next to an idiot if he write in support of the Ministry from whom he hopes to receive it : he ought to attack them with all his weapons, and he will soon attract their attention : as a friend, he would be insignificant and unnoticed, like the gnat in the spurious poem attributed to Virgil ; but even a gnat, as an enemy, is formidable, and means must be taken to get rid of him. So with young Lawyers ; if they start on the ministerial side in politics, they are passed over and neglected : though they seize every occasion to extol and eulogize, their pains will be thrown away; but let them begin life as opponents to the men in power, and in case of a change of Ministry they stand fair for rewards, and in case of no change they are marked men to be tempted with the first offer that is likely to be successful.

Whatever contempt I may feel for the conduct of Mr. Sergeant COPLEY as a politician, it is impossible for me to feel any thing like contempt for his talents as an Advocate :

they certainly are of the first rank, and wel
entitle him even to a larger share of busines
than he at present enjoys. I well recollect
before he was made a Sergeant, feeling a
conviction that he could command success
and would ere many years had elapsed be a
the head of his profession : my principa
doubt was which would take the lead, the
present Attorney General or Mr. COPLEY
although they are men whose minds are of a
different structure, and therefore in some res
pects not to be compared together : the at
tainments of the former are, I apprehend
much more deep-laid and solid, and Sir R
Gifford has besides a more logical and argu
mentative head; but in legal learning, Mr
Sergeant COPLEY is not thought by any mean
deficient, and his opinion is always listened
to with deference by the Bench : but he is a
man of labour, and his knowledge does no
appear to be very applicable on a sudden : he
requires more time for research and arrange
ment when he is entrusted with an argument;
and although it may be very learned, and the
points generally well disposed, it has not that

perfect symmetry and proportion of all the parts, like an architectural structure, for which he exertions of Sir R. Gifford in this kind are very remarkable: the Attorney-General has besides a most admirable method of putting a point, which of itself is sometimes equal to an argument, and renders the task of enforcing and illustrating almost unnecessary. Yet if Mr. Sergeant COPLEY's acquaintance with the more complicated and difficult branches of the law be not so profound and systematic, his knowledge upon other matters extremely useful to an Advocate, is much more extensive and varied. I hardly know a man at the Bar who avails himself so often of the advantage afforded by a regular education, and by reading, not confined to the mere dry pursuit in which he is engaged: he is much more than a Lawyer, which I believe Sir R. Gifford is not: he is apparently well read, not only in the historians but in the poets of his country, at least in such as come within the reach of individuals who have not made the *belles lettres* their main study. On this account, at *Nisi Prius* he shines with peculiar brightness in

contrast with the prosings of the late Attorney-
General, or the arrogant ignorance of Mr.
Sergeant Vaughan.—Owen Feltham, in his
Resolves, well says that "arrogance is a weed
that ever grows upon a dunghill;" and Mr. Sergeant Vaughan is one more proof of the truth
of the assertion. With sufficient confidence in
his own strength and powers, (which is far removed from presumptuousness, and without
which no man will be successful at the Bar,
and scarcely in any other situation) Mr. Sergeant COPLEY is not without diffidence towards such as he ought to acknowledge his
superiors: it would be next to impossible for
any man but Mr. Sergeant Vaughan to treat
his Brother Lens with disrespect: and Mr.
Sergeant COPLEY, when I have had an opportunity of seeing them engaged on opposite
sides, always shews a remarkable degree of
deference and regard for Mr. Sergeant Lens
and his opinions: there can scarcely be a
stronger contrast than between a cause mana
ged by Sergeants Best and Vaughan and by
Sergeants Lens and COPLEY. I do not say
that I have not heard Mr. Sergeant COPLEY

when employed against other antagonists, violent and perhaps coarse in his expressions, but not until he was compelled to combat them with their own weapons, and to meet their occasional vulgarity by a retort which, besides its coarseness, frequently had severe sarcasm or keen wit to recommend and redeem it.

Notwithstanding I think highly both of the talents and attainments of the subject of the present article, as a speaker he is by no means all that could be wished : perhaps the best, and the best known, specimen was given by him as one of the Counsel for *Watson* on his trial for high treason ; and it was in the mouths of all who heard it, that it was delivered with almost unintelligible velocity : his volubility is excessive, and indeed this is the greatest fault of his addresses : on that occasion it was said in excuse, that as his leader Mr. Wetherell had occupied so much time, he felt it his duty to compress as far as possible, and to include a great deal of matter in small compass. To a certain extent the remark

might be just, and it may be true also, as
believe it is, that he always has some persua
sion of the kind upon his mind: he neve
appeals to a Jury without talking infinitely
too fast, by which he not only loses his impressiveness, but his hearers have scarcely
time to reflect for a moment upon one position
before they are hurried on to another. Be i
remembered, too, that he seldom offers any
thing that is frivolous or unnecessary—no
thing that does not mainly conduce to the
point at which he is aiming. Of course thi
excessive rapidity prevents the due emphasi
and force that ought to be given to particular
words, and on this account some would fairly
enough complain of a degree of monotony ir
his delivery. With all this injurious rapidity, however, which it would be supposed
must unavoidably interfere with precision
Mr. Sergeant COPLEY's periods are formed
not only with correctness, but with great nicety and exactness : his sentences are frequently
long—too long for perspicuousness—but they
are not involved in parentheses, and are always complete : each is well constructed,

with a due relation and proportion in the clauses—and they are not by any means deficient in variety, which is the common error of those who are not interrogatory and colloquial speakers. On the whole, what he says is better to be read than to be heard; and if the stenographic art could exactly follow him, very little alteration and correction would be required before his speeches were given to the printer.

It must be allowed, that Mr. Sergeant COPLEY's manner is not the most happy: as there is a little monotony in his voice, there is a great deal of it (if I may so say) in his look; for the expression of his countenance is nearly always the same; his brow is somewhat scowling, and he has that kind of forehead which a physiognomist would say indicated great foresight and penetration; so that his eye is overshadowed; more especially as the light is usually managed in our Courts in Westminster, where it falls directly upon the top of the head, and gives a heavy shade to the whole countenance. His action is also wanting in variety: he makes but little use of either arm, and almost none at all of the left: the right, when employed, is commonly only swayed up and down in a sort of time-beating mode, and the principal use of it seems to be to mark when the speaker arrives at particular divisions or points of his sentence. If he argues a point of law or any other matter requiring precision, the fore-finger of his right-hand is called into very frequent employment. He generally keeps his figure in quite an erect posture, which is a degree or two better than the habit some Barristers have acquired of swaying backwards and forwards like a blind singer in the street.

There is no part of the duty of an Advocate in which Mr. Sergeant COPLEY is more dexterous than in the discussion of a point of evidence while a witness is in the box: he possesses considerable acuteness and great ingenuity, and he appears more at home upon the law of this subject than some others: they are matters rather of nicety than of research. As an instance, I would mention his struggle

against the disclosure of certain official com-
munications in a cause of Thorpe *v.* the
Governor of Upper Canada*.   He is also a
very shrewd and close examiner of a witness,
but he has not the knack of throwing him off
his guard by that appearance of unconcern
which Lord Erskine used so successfully to
assume; for Mr. Sergeant COPLEY always
seems too intent upon what is about to fall
from the witness to put on any disguise of
that sort.

* On this occasion, Lord Castlereagh was present on
the Bench, and seemed much gratified by the display of
talent on the part of Mr. Sergeant COPLEY: not long afterwards the latter came into Parliament.

MR. JERVIS AND MR. RAINE.

Nomen habet, et ad magistri
Vocem quisquis sui venit citatus.

Mart. L. 4. E. 30.

WITH respect to the two gentlemen whose
names stand at the head of the present article,
I am much in the situation of the person
of whom Montaigne speaks, when he says
(*Essais*, L. II. chap. 14) " *C'est une plai-
sante imagination de concevoir un esprit ba-
lancé justement entre deux pareilles envies ;'*
for it is really a matter of some difficulty with
me to decide with which of them I shall begin :
the same lively and facetious author goes on
to illustrate what he advances, by supposing
a man between a ham and a bottle, *avec egal
appetit de boire et de manger ;* which is again
something like my case; for one of the individuals, whose merits or defects are under

discussion, in several particulars may be said to resemble a ham, and the other a bottle, if not of small beer, assuredly not of the briskest and brightest Champaigne. For instance, Mr. RAINE may be considered both salt and savoury, though now and then too coarse and too high; and Mr. JERVIS is not unlike a bottle of table-ale, with but little body and fulness, but with much of the spirit and uppishness, if I may so say without any reference to temper, belonging to more generous and intoxicating liquor: at the same time, the flavour is not unpleasant, and it may and does go down very well in places where they are more thirsty, or have tastes less sophisticated, than in the metropolis, or (to quit my simile) where speeches are not so plentiful. But the question is, with whom I shall begin, and though the usual course is to eat before we drink, I shall here reverse the order of things, and commence with Mr. JERVIS, because he claims precedence on the ground of seniority :

Dum in dubio est animus, paulo momento huc, illuc impellitur.—*Ter. Andr.* A. 1, Sc, 5.

He obtained a silk gown, by patent of precedence, when his uncle, Lord St. Vincent, was at the head of the Admiralty, and from the mere mention of this circumstance, it will perhaps be concluded that Mr. JERVIS's merits only did not entitle him to this distinction—a distinction which very few King's Counsel enjoy; for the patent of precedence gives him an advantage over his rivals, because he can undertake the defence of a person accused of any crime and prosecuted by the Crown, without the expensive licence that must otherwise be obtained. It is to be taken for granted, indeed, that a little ministerial and family influence was employed, since the talents and qualifications of Mr. JERVIS are by no means such as to enable him to extort honours and command business. Yet let me in the outset make a remark, in which I shall be confirmed by nearly the whole Bar, that he has always had to work up hill in the profession : he never has possessed the ear of the Court of King's Bench, and if he has ever succeeded in convincing the minds of

s

the Judges, it has been by overcoming difficulties and repelling objections quite as frequently started and supported by the highest
authorities, as by the Counsel who were opposed to him : that both sides have been
heard cannot be denied ; but one side was
heard principally from the Bench, the other
from the Bar. Mr. JERVIS, however, possesses both patience and perseverance, and if
he be not the closest reasoner in the world,
he can make an argument intelligible ; and
without shewing disrespect to the Court, I
have sometimes seen him much more laud-
ably pertinacious, than men of higher talents
but of more timidity. I have several times
had occasion to protest against the tame submissiveness which some advocates are not
ashamed to expose in public ; but this praise
is, I think, above all due to Mr. JERVIS, that
he more correctly than any other man draws
the line between that deference which is due
to superiors, and that mental degradation
which is due to no man. Whether the unusual obstacles he experienced in the Court

of King's Bench led to the determination, or whether it was induced by a prospect of additional business, I know not; but within the last three or four terms he has confined his practice almost exclusively to the Court of Exchequer, where, in consequence of his patent, he is enabled to conduct the defence of such persons as, chiefly in revenue causes, are prosecuted by the Attorney-General. For this reason, his name is not now so familiar with the public as it used to be when he sat in that Court, the proceedings of which are almost exclusively reported in the newspapers: he only appears there now, when his presence is required in consequence of some proceeding arising out of country business.

On the Oxford circuit, however, there is no man better known or better liked : his chief rival was Mr. Dauncey, of whom I spoke in a preceding article; and if the latter were thought the abler man, the former was considered by far the most gentlemanly advocate, and was much more approved if not admired

s 2

both by suitors and solicitors: he and Mr.
Dauncey generally divided the practice, one
being engaged on one side and the other on
the other, though of the two Mr. Dauncey
certainly had the advantage. In my criticism upon this latter gentleman, I mentioned
that he was a great talker, and I added, what
is liable to misinterpretation, and has in fact
been misinterpreted, that Mr. JERVIS could
talk a little: I ought rather to have said,
that he was a moderate talker: he speaks
nearly as fast and as long as Mr. Dauncey was
in the habit of doing, but he never ventures to
take the same liberties with his cause or his
auditory; he endeavours to talk to the purpose, and does not travel out of his road in
all directions merely because he thinks himself
vastly entertaining.*   The great objection to
be made to Mr. JERVIS's addresses is, that
there is such a laxity about them, such a want
of coherence of parts, a want of nerve, sinew,
and tension: he does not say bad things, so
much as he puts them in bad places; he does

* It ought to be remembered that this comparison was
made nearly a year before the death of Mr. Dauncey.

not arrange and digest what he has to offer, and
he does not succeed in making his points tell
in consequence of a looseness of phraseology
and a want of precision, vigour, and strength
in his language.　For this reason he sometimes
fails to secure the attention of the Jury, who
are weary of following him from one end of the
cause to the other, and from one fact to another, without order or system, long before he
arrives at the conclusion of what he feels it
his duty to offer.　Yet he is by no means an
inelegant speaker—indeed he seems to have
studied his manner and appearance; and as he
is a gentleman in his conduct and in his feelings, he never launches out into the gross abuse
and needless coarseness closely bordering upon
vulgarity; for which his more immediate rival
on the circuit was sometimes celebrated.　He
always seems deeply interested for his client,
without measuring the exact proportion it
ought to bear to the fee he has received.

One advantage Mr. JERVIS possesses over
Counsel who are in other respects his superiors, is a great command of his temper : he

s 3

is not easily ruffled or thrown off his guard, and he can bear a joke, even though it be not of the most polished kind, with equanimity. On this account, he is able sometimes to cope with an insolent witness when other men would make appeals to the Court for protection : mere impudence is very easily baffled by a man of coolness and quickness, even if his talents be not of the first order : into this coolness and controul over himself he has been tolerably disciplined in the Court of King's Bench, where, as I remarked, I have often seen them put to a very severe test : he is naturally of a mild, tranquil deportment, and such men usually display sufficient firmness when the occasion demands it. I do not apprehend that he has any pretensions to be considered a profound lawyer, and he does not attempt to plume himself upon attainments he does not possess.

Of Mr. RAINE, I am aware that very little is known in the metropolis : he is, I believe, the son of the late head master of the Charter House, and he bears the reputation among

his friends of being a good scholar : it may
be true, and very likely is so ; but no man
who had ever heard him speak would have
supposed that he had even a slight acquaintance with classic or any other literature.
Though he very seldom obtains a brief in
London, he is a very constant attendant in
his place in Court, where his absence would of
late often have been more convenient, in consequence of the crowded state of the table from
the recent batches of King's Counsel. But
if his absence would be more convenient,
it would not be more agreeable, for he is
reckoned a most good-natured man, and dis-
tributes his puns and his franks (as a member
of Parliament) among his surrounding friends
with great liberality : the former are the more
plentiful, and the latter usually the more ac-
ceptable : his wit is not very discriminating
nor fastidious, and he has seldom resolution
to let an occasion slip on which he can torture
some poor word into a double signification.
Although this is his chief occupation in Westminster-Hall, I have seen him now and then
engaged in a cause, where he might have

distinguished himself had he chosen to do so; he did not however appear to think it worth while to give himself any trouble, and scarcely to take the most ordinary pains in the opening of the facts and in the examination of the witnesses. He was in some degree in the right, for had he exerted himself ever so much, and been ever so much approved, he would probably now come into the field too late in the day, when the ground is occupied by more popular rivals.

This is not by any means the case upon the Northern Circuit, where Mr. RAINE is employed by many of the country attornies : here he has established, to a certain extent, a reputation, and he endeavours to keep it up, and to make a further progress, by doing his utmost for such as entrust him with their briefs : this therefore is the proper situation for measuring his talents, while a very erroneous standard would be formed from his practice in London.

It may easily be supposed, that Mr. Top-

ping and Mr. Scarlett engross a very great
proportion of the business: they are commonly adversaries; but now and then a rich
and cunning suitor will take care to retain
both of them in his favour, and then Mr
RAINE is employed to oppose them, probably with the assistance of Mr. Sergeant
Hullock, a hard-headed, straight-forward
north-countryman, with a very strong brogue
and as strong an understanding. Mr. RAINE
however leads, as considerably senior, and I
have heard him on such occasions make very
strenuous and effective speeches: in some of
the country towns he is preferred by a few
even to the two great men of the circuit, and
it cannot be denied that he has with a certain
class, what the knowing ones term, a taking
way with him: he is undoubtedly very
shrewd, and in causes not obviously above
his capacity he acquits himself to the satisfaction of all parties, and not least to his
own: without being presumptuous or assum-
ing, it is obvious, when he has gained
verdict or made a good address, that he sits
down in very good humour with himself

It is notorious, I believe, that in Yorkshir
there are more horse-dealers than in any othe
county in England; and as horse-dealer
are usually also skilful in the pugilistic art
it follows that at the Assizes the causes re
garding horses and assaults are tolerably nu
merous. Now to do Mr. RAINE justice, :
do not think that there is a man at the Bar
who knows how to conduct a horse-cause
better than himself, who is more up to the
tricks of the trade, and to the manœuvre
it is necessary to practise. Actions relating
to insurances on shipping are now generally
considered a distinct branch of the profession, and those that are connected with the
soundness or unsoundness of horses ought
almost to be looked upon in the same light:
they are quite distinct in their nature from
other suits, and distinct principles and precedents are applicable to them. Mr. RAINE
seems to have made them his peculiar study,
and they are seldom brought before a Jury
without his being retained either for the plaintiff or the defendant. He has the terms of art
and slang of the stable at his tongue's end,

so as to make himself easily intelligible to the witnesses, and if they prevaricate or commit perjury (which is by no means uncommon he possesses considerable art in their manage- ment or detection. He has a most knowing look, and a shake of the head, when he rises to cross-examine, or when he does not obtain a direct answer to a question, which alarms even a practised witness, and makes him be- lieve that the advocate is much more in the secret than he is in reality. To the Jury also he appears so scientific, so well ac- quainted with the subject, that they cannot but hesitate in deciding against his judgment.

He is certainly a forcible and a pointed speaker, but most unselect in his phraseology, and very careless about offending the ears of his auditory, by vulgarisms and expressions that may be very proper when talking to a witness in his own language, but are alto- gether misplaced in a speech : he addresses himself to the question, and argues in a plain, though in an acute and often convincing stile. With regard to his classical attainments, I

m not aware, as I have said, that he ever
gives his audience the slightest glimpse of
hem. What he may be in private, I know
not ; but judging from his public life, I
hould be inclined to say, that elegant learn-
ng was never more completely thrown away.

SIR SAMUEL ROMILLY.

"A piercing wit quite void of ostentation; high-erected thoughts seated in a heart of courtesy; an eloquence as sweet in the uttering, as slow to come to the uttering.—*Sir P. Sidney's Arcadia.*

I HAVE hitherto postponed all mention of Sir SAMUEL ROMILLY, from an unfeigned diffidence in my own powers to do his talents justice : at length the time has arrived, when such a task is unhappily a tribute to the dead, not a criticism upon the living ; if before I felt my own incompetence and shrunk from the undertaking, how doubly difficult must I feel it now, and how reluctant must I be to avail myself of this last opportunity of speaking of an individual, regarding

T

whom every sentence I utter must be accompanied by the reflection, that his eloquence, his learning, and his zeal in the cause of humanity, are lost to the world for ever!*

Yet even here we have our consolation ; however deeply we may regret that his bene_volent and beneficent existence is terminated, we can say, that had it been more protracted, he could probably have effected no more than

* Of course I meant in his person, for some of the fruits of his labours are now ripening in other hands. At the time this article was published, I was in hopes that some attempt would be made to collect and publish the speeches of Sir S. ROMILLY in Parliament with a selection of those delivered in his professional capacity. In both cases, perhaps, some discretion might be necessary, as his addresses were not all equally well reported, nor were the subjects always of general interest. Finding that the task was undertaken by nobody else, I had commenced it myself, but was discouraged by the little interest that seemed to be taken by the public in what concerned this distinguished and most benevolent individual, after his decease. It is singular, that in Parliament only two passing allusions were made to the loss the country had sustained. Silent-sorrow and admiration, if they exist, are always liable to misapprehension : public grief cannot well be too ostentatious, for the sake of public example.

he lived to accomplish. One great object o
his political exertions was a wise and tempe
rate reform; but he well knew that upon suc
a subject in the House of Commons he talke
to those who would not hear or could no
understand—who trembled at every little in
road of knowledge, and whose security an
stability depended upon keeping in ignoranc
the great mass of the people. But Sir SAMUE
ROMILLY survived to see a free spirit of en
quiry active among all classes, and by hin
that free spirit was at least animated and en
couraged, if not raised and created; its progress may be slow, but it must be certain
and though this generation may not witnes
its final triumph, yet the purpose may b
said to have been attained in the present ag
for the benefit of posterity. In the abolition
of that horrid traffic, which made a profit
not merely of the lives, but of the groans and
agonies of our fellow creatures, be mainly
assisted. His attempts to purge our pena
code of some of its barbarous and useles
absurdities will never be forgotten, and hi
ill success will serve to perpetuate the dis-

grace of those who resisted his efforts with
a pertinacious and uninformed senselessness,
almost equal to that with which some of the
measures originated : ignorance and prejudice are antagonists that time alone can overcome.   He set the example, and though it
may not be effectually followed, his exertions
were at least persevering, if they were not
successful.

With regard to personal aggrandisement,
he had nothing left to wish : title and office
would have diminished instead of adding to
his reputation : to be Chancellor would have
been less than to be ROMILLY.

It is said by one of our eloquent early
writers, in his sententious way, that " as a
great body is not without a like shadow, so
eminent virtue is not without eminent detrac-
tion—calumny should die with the carcase
of her subject ;* but in reference to ROMILLY,
she never lived ; her putrid breath never tainted

* A. Stafford's Niobé, 1611.

his fame ; and though he might be envie
by a few low-minded wretches, they wei
too dastardly to avow themselves his enemies
and too mean to be numbered among hi
friends : he was revered at the Bar, admire
in the Senate, and beloved by the People
he was of no party in heart, and only of
party in act, because he knew that single an
unsupported endeavours could occomplisl
nothing : he seldom spoke without excitin;
dumb attention in his hearers, and enthusiasti
admiration in his country : no man ever darec
to doubt the purity of his motives, and h
often compelled reluctant conviction by th
force and soundness of his reasoning. "
have conversed with some men (observe
Jeremy Taylor) who rejoiced in the death o
calamity of others, and accounted it as i
judgment upon them for being on the othei
side and against them in the contention ;'
but to no one, however heartless from party
feelings, and however uncharitable from political animosities, can such a remark in the
present instance be applied. It was delightful to see how all persons of all opinions,

united in one feeling of admiration, and it is still delightful to observe how they all unite in one feeling of regret.

Although the common-places of condolence are in the mouths of every one, and although upon an occasion like this little can be said but common-places, yet in sitting down to form as nearly as I can a fair estimate of the merits and defects of Sir SAMUEL ROMILLY, uninfluenced by any thing but a recollection of what they were, I could not avoid a few words to lament that I must now say of them that *they were.*

He had been long at the head of the Chancery Bar ; for though he was not the senior King's Counsel, Sir A. Piggot taking precedence, yet in point of talent and extent of business he was far above competition : he was *facile princeps* in that Court, and was concerned in almost every important question that came before it. The presiding Judge, remarkable for his timorous and mistaken diffidence, always listened to him with the utmost attention, and if he saw that Sir SAMUEL ROMILLY, independent of his capacity as an advocate, was of a different opinion to that which he had formed upon any question, he scarcely dared to decide against him, nor would he at last venture to do so, until the force of the argument had by time been worn away. Though in one point of view this might be of advantage to his clients, it was very detrimental to his own interests, for the eternal postponement of decisions prevented the rapid progress of business: on the other hand, Sir SAMUEL ROMILLY was harrassed by attornies and parties, who hour by hour besieged him to read their briefs, to answer their cases, or to bring forward matters, which if mentioned could not have been heard, and if heard would not have been determined. Notwithstanding, he was probably in the receipt of a larger income than was ever before acquired by any member of the profession; and it is known that at some periods of the year his table was so heaped with cases on which his opinion was desired, that he was obliged at last to close his doors, and to clear away the accumulated mass before he allowed any more to collect. The load of business he had to dismiss must, on such occasions, have been extremly oppressive; and it would not be surprising if the vast arrear that must have been occasioned by his close attendance on his wife, and the knowledge that if he recovered his strength he should have to wade through it with a mind worn down and distracted by an overbearing calamity, had partially contributed to the temporary derangement which had so fatal a consequence. Yet his industry, when in health and spirits, was astonishing; it appeared before the Coroner that he usually rose at six, and though by nature fitted for the delights and comforts of a domestic circle, and for the intercourse of social life, he saw but little of his family or his friends. But these privations, at first no doubt reluctantly endured, at length became habitual. There is sufficient evidence to shew that though he might originally embrace the profession of the law with some degree of love for the pursuit, yet of late years, had it been possible for him to have limited more the amount of his business, he would have relieved himself from a considerable part of the burden he was under the painful necessity of continuing to sustain. His perseverance was accompanied by a quickness of apprehension equalled by very few, because perhaps very few have an opportunity of bringing it to such a degree of perfection: his memory too was proportionably retentive, and it was really sometimes wonderful to see him open brief after brief, and, almost without references, or even marks to guide his eye and direct his attention, detail to the Chancellor with the utmost precision the complicated facts they contained.—In another respect, also, it was extremely obvious; for where he was called upon to reply, whether in Court or in Parliament, he made few or no notes of the speeches of his antagonists. In one way, however, this was attended with disadvantages, as I shall presently explain.

These are to be considered not as peculiar gifts, but in some degree as acquirements, which others might attain with the same means ; but who by any practice, by any industry however laborious, shall attain that elegant, that refined, that persuasive, yet, at times that nervous and forcible eloquence, in which he has never been exceeded, I doubt if ever equalled, by any lawyer in any age.

I remarked in a previous paper, that in Chancery of all our Courts there is least room for a display of the powers of language: independent of impediments I then referred to, the Advocates there have generally too much to do to attempt any thing of the kind, and this was especially the case with Sir SAMUEL ROMILLY; yet in transacting the most ordinary business there was a peculiar grace about his manner—a gentlemanly ease, an unpresuming suavity, that won the hearts of all his hearers. There are some men who sit in that Court and enjoy a certain share of business, whose excellence is quite of a negative kind—who are content with never doing any thing positively well, provided they never do any thing absolutely ill : to this class of course Sir SAMUEL ROMILLY did not belong, and on important occasions, when more exertion and study was required, there was nothing like effort in what fell from him : his most graceful sentences flowed from his lips without pomp or ostentation, as if the words he used, however apt and forcible, dropped naturally and inartificially into their places, without the application either of will or memory. How often have we been disgusted with speakers for their obtrusive attempts to employ round and sonorious phraseology ; but with him it seemed as if the last thing he cared about was the precise mode in which he expressed his thoughts; so much so, that the chief fault of his addresses, both in and out of Parliament, was sometimes a want of force and selectness in the terms he employed : he carried his love of simplicity and his hatred of affectation to an injudicious extreme. For the same reason, he took very little pains about the frame and construction of his sentences ; they were never formed upon any rule or system, but their force and beauty were derived, either from

he inspiration of the subject, or from the
natural grace that always accompanied their
delivery One faculty was possessed by Sir
SAMUEL ROMILLY above all competition—
that of never deviating from the point in
question; and this is the more remarkable,
because in the multifariousness of his avocations he must have been frequently called
upon to speak on the spur of the moment,
when comparatively unprepared : it never
could be said of him, that he wasted time by
unnecessary or frivolous remarks, or dwelt
upon matters of little importance to the issue:
he always kept the great question in view as
a land-mark, and arrived at it by the nearest
possible road.

But if he were admirable as a juridical,
he was more so as a parliamentary, orator,
and in this respect, accomplished much more
than any professed practical lawyer I ever
heard or read of. I have already taken occasion to complain of the stile of speaking
almost invariably adopted by Barristers who
obtained seats in the House of Commons—

a petty, haggling, quibbling, punctilious stile, if I may so say, which dwells only upon un-influencing details, and oppositions of paltry discrepancies. Sir SAMUEL ROMILLY, on the contrary, always took up a subject upon the broadest grounds of public policy, and em-braced the most extended views of its causes, consequences, and bearings; his mind could never descend to littleness, and in his practice at the Bar, he much oftener took his stand upon principles than upon precedents ; or, in referring to the latter, he seldom failed to shew how far they were established upon the former. But this general mode of discussing a question in Parliament was the effect of necessity, as well as of natural inclination : could he, who from six in the morning until the hour when he entered the House had been unceasingly em-ployed in his professional occupations, have time to study the *minutiæ* and inferior details of a subject—to pick out particular facts and coincidences ? On this account, very few debates originated with him, excepting upon topics incidently connected with his pursuit ; on other occasions, he commonly spoke in reply, and not unfrequently at so late an hour of the night, that what he said found its way very imperfectly into the newspapers. For this reason, I should fear that it will be difficult to form a tolerable collection of his speeches for separate publication.

He was by no means always equally forcible ; and though extremely energetic, when roused or warmed by his subject, there was at times in Parliament a feebleness of voice and language, partly to be accounted for by the easy conversational mode in which business is conducted in the Court where he practised : this gave him in some degree that carelessness of phraseology, and that irregularity in the construction of his sentences, I before noticed, aided by his obvious disgust at any thing approaching ostentatious pretence. I do not think that he was remarkable for a logical or lucid arrangement of his subject, nor for any artifice, common to practised speakers, of putting his strongest points in the fittest places. When answering an opponent, I have often felt that he adverted to the arguments in a manner too desultory—just as they presented themselves to his recollection : had he taken more notes, this defect perhaps might have been remedied; yet I admit that too many notes only serve to distract and confuse. His general deportment was mild and candid, and if he were not always so affable or communicative in private as many persons wished, it did not arise from any haughtiness of disposition, but from the anxiously burdened state of his mind : he who had not time for social or domestic intercourse, could feel but little inclination to waste it upon tedious talk and unmeaning compliments.

I have thus attempted to draw the character of Sir SAMUEL ROMILLY as an Advocate and as a Senator, and my principal fear is, that in endeavouring to shun the ordinary cant, I have spoken of him less favourably in some points than I should have done had he yet been living.——The deference paid to his opinions by every member of the profession, speaks all that can be said in favour of his legal knowledge; the delighted attention with which he was heard in the House of Commons, even when the members were worn out by the fatigues of a long debate, is sufficient testimony of his powers as a parliamentary orator; and the ardent attachment of his family, his friends, and his domestics, shews that the brightness of his talents did not exceed the kindness and benignity of his nature:—

" His ruins, like the sacred carcases
Of scattered temples, great and reverend lie,
And the religious honour them no less
Than if they stood in all their gallantry."

Daniel's Philotas, A. 5.

MR. WETHERELL.

None other council good him seemeth
But such as himself deemeth:
For in such wise as he compasseth,
His wit alone all other passeth,***
And weeneth of him selven so,
That such as he is there be no'mo.

Gower's Conf. Am. L. I.

In the course of my remarks upon those who practise at the English Bar, I have necessarily interwoven some few strictures upon what may be considered abuses or defects in the proceedings of our Courts of Justice; there is one however very obvious to all who have closely attended, but with which the public in general are little acquainted, and to which I have not yet adverted—I mean the vast expence of Government Prosecutions: no reference is here intended to *ex-officio* in-

ormations for State libels, nor to indictments
or great crimes, but to proceedings in the
King's Bench against insignificant offenders
—such as those who commit assaults upon,
or obstruct, revenue officers, or those who
gainst the statute are discovered to have
aval stores in their possession : the former are
ery numerous, and the latter by no means un-
requent.   Some have argued that these petty
delinquents ought to be tried and punished
t the Sessions—that the same rule that applies to a case of private outrage (in which
he Court often observes, that justice would
ave been satisfied without the needless and
heavy expense of removal by *certiorari*,)
ought to be extended to prosecutions of this
kind.   I do not enter into this question, which
may admit of difference of opinion on the
ground that at the Sessions petty Juries will
ot convict upon such charges; but what I
omplain of is, that when they are brought
orward in the Court of King's Bench an
mmense expense is incurred, which is wholly
useless, and might therefore be avoided.
Whether more witnesses are summoned and

paid for than are necessary, or whether in
the working of the indictment, (if I may
borrow a phrase from bankruptcy,) more
money is expended by the Solicitors for the
Excise, Customs, or the Admiralty, I do no
know, and I do not inquire: I protest here
only against the employment, with very heavy
fees, of a whole row of King's Counsel, when
less than the talents and experience enjoyed
by any one of them would be quite sufficien
to ensure a conviction; especially when we
recollect that such matters are always tried
by a Special Jury, never much disposed to
favour a poor smuggler who defends the pro
perty he has actually paid for, or the wretched
chandler, in whose cellar has been found a
rope's end with the white twine in the centre
or a copper bolt marked with the broad
arrow. Every barrister, of only a few years
standing, must have observed many instance
of this kind. A remarkable proof of th
correctness of what I state occurred only
few sittings ago, when an unhappy Jew
broker, I think he was, residing somewhere
in Wapping, was indicted for having in hi

possession some pieces of metal, without the needful document to prove their purchase at the King's sale; he made no defence, I believe employed no advocate, and the fact was proved against him by one or at most two credible witnesses, yet not less than five counsel were retained by the Crown against him, four of them with silk-gowns, and of course receiving nearly double fees. I need not enumerate their names, more particularly as they themselves (as if they felt some sense of the impropriety of receiving so much money for doing absolutely nothing, not even for reading their briefs,) seemed anxious to keep in the back ground, and not to appear to have any thing to do with the proceeding. As I said before, without entering into any examination of the preliminary proceedings, (which I really am not competent to do) if they are conducted upon the same system, and by the same scale, the charge upon the public is enormously beyond what it ought to bear. I may here notice what I consider another abuse, though perhaps of less magnitude: if my information be correct, and I have no reason to doubt it, the Attorney and Solicitor-General each receives a large fee upon every prosecution brought to trial in the Exchequer, even though they have had nothing to do with it in its progress, and left the management as leader entirely to Mr. Dauncey or Mr. Clarke.* The motives for this unwarrantable expenditure of public money is the same in both cases—to keep up the influence of the Crown and its Ministers —to lead King's Counsel always to be expecting something, and to induce them to avoid all opportunities of giving umbrage to those in power.

I have had the less reluctance in making these remarks in a free spirit, because on this occasion they cannot be supposed to have an invidious or personal application : the individual whose capacity and qualifications are before us in the present article, confines

---

* In this Court also many more counsel are largely feed, in every case relating to the revenue, than are at all necessary. A very considerable saving might be made by the correction of this abuse even here.

his practice almost solely to Courts of Equity, and can therefore have no concern or connection with trials such as those to which I have adverted.

The name of Mr. WETHERELL was pretty generally known even before he obtained a silk-gown, for his practice was considerable not only in the Courts of Chancery and Exchequer, but before Committees of both Houses of Parliament: his advancement in his profession, and his obtaining a seat in the House of Commons, contributed still further to bring him into public notice, and his volunteered defence of *Watson* and others, when tried for high treason, drew all eyes upon him : some wondering how it happened that he of all men at the Bar should step forward on such an occasion, and others doubting how he would fulfil the task he had thus unexpectedly undertaken. Into his private motives I shall not enter ; whether they originated in political pique at not being made Solicitor - General in preference to Sir R. Gifford, or in a love of notoriety and popularity, I shall not investigate : I have only to do here with the proportion of talent, knowledge, and zeal, he displayed upon that occasion, and with his general abilities and merits as an advocate.

Whether he did or did not feel rancorously against ministers, certain it is, that he acted strenuously for those who were accused by them : he exerted himself to the utmost, and what is much more important (for more than half the world measure the means by the end) his exertions were successful :—he obtained a verdict of acquittal, and he made a speech of more than eight hours duration. · Even the last circumstance, with a great number of people, would have obtained him the title of an orator, and I must remark, that during the greater part of the time, to such persons he seemed to address himself. Not a few of those who did not hear him, (and how few could, on account of the smallness of the Court,) will think this observation severe— perhaps unjust ; they read his speech in the newspapers, and from that source they judged

f its merits; they thought it, no doubt, as
good as the case admitted—in some parts
acute, in others learned, and as a whole forcible if not convincing.   They are not aware of
he infinite repetitions with which it abounded,
of the tedious length to which some of the
weakest points were spun out, and of the
flimsey vapidness of most of those portions
where Mr. WETHERELL attempted to be
eloquent and to rouse the feelings of the
jury.   The beginning of his harangue consisted chiefly of state quotations from trite
books, and mistaken positions of law with
all the pretence of learning; and the end, of
pompous declamation,—at least as pompous
is the speaker's paucity, or more properly,
little variety of words and phraseology, could
make it:

————————————————All in fustian suit
Is clothed a huge nothing—all for the repute
Of profound knowledge.
J. Marston's Sc. of Villany, L. 3.

I think I might securely appeal to every
judicious and impartial auditor, whether the
speech did not deserve this character: I say

impartial auditor, because I believe that among a few of the seniors of the King's Bench Bar, a little envy prevailed, and prevented them from forming quite a fair estimate:* Mr. WETHERELL had travelled out of his Court, and he certainly shewed that he was not very familiar with the subject of which he was treating; he wanted much of the skill and readiness which a *nisi prius* advocate ought to possess. Had he not received most able assistance from Mr. Sergeant Copley, upon technical matters and points of evidence, he would probably have appeared to the nation at large much more incompetent than he was actually considered. His other co-adjutors, (if indeed the term can be properly applied to them,) Messrs. E. Lawes,

---

* It is obvious that a speech of eight hours could not be given in a newspaper, and the consequence was, that Mr. WETHERELL's address to the Jury underwent a great deal of wholesome pruning: all the sappy exuberant branches were lopped off, and the dead wood cut out: so that with a small addition of force and vigour in the vapid parts, and many omissions of re-statements, it made a much more respectable figure in print than in Court. But in these observations let not the difficulty and novelty of the undertaking be forgotten.

x

Holt, Rigby, and Starkie, did little else but take most laborious notes from the beginning to the end of the trial, and for this duty I do not deny that they were all exceedingly competent. But dismissing Mr. WETHERELL's address from discussion, which it is not improbable many readers have long ago dismissed from their memories, it may be fit that I should say a word or two respecting the celebrated cross-examination of the infamous *Castles:* here it was thought, by all but those who were most competent to judge, that the advocate acquitted himself with the greatest ability: it went out to the world, that by dint of worming insinuation and dexterous artifice, the Counsel had extracted from the witness facts most damning to his character and credibility. I do not pretend to say that some ingenuity was not displayed now and then in the mode in which a question was worded; not to put the truth point blank, and thus to tempt a point blank denial, but to offer it in such a moderated form, as led the person in the box to suppose that no great injury could arise from admitting the fact to that extent:

in this respect some skill was shown, but Mr. WETHERELL did not succeed in a single point upon which he had not already obtained the full particulars from his brief. He rather failed in proving all he expected, than prevailed in establishing more than he was instructed: that only is a cross-examination meriting the highest praise due to such an effort, where the advocate from some glimmering hint, perhaps let fall by the witness himself, proceeds step by step to the developement of a whole system of falsehood and iniquity.

It remains for me to speak of Mr. WETHERELL as a Counsel in Courts of Equity, which, as I have said, is the sphere to which he confines his practice: I do not think that before the trial of *Watson* and others he had quitted it for many years. Here he indulges his passion for talking quite as freely as upon the occasion above referred to; I mean, of course, taking into consideration the comparative importance of the cases: he always seems to me to say about twice as

iuch, or to speak more precisely, to utter
early twice as many words, as are necessary
pon any question. He runs on with vast
olubility from fact to fact, and from point
▸ point, and with so little arrangement, that
is repetitions are innumerable and weari-
ɔme: while he is adverting to one topic,
nother strikes him, and he instantly flies off
t a tangent to it; and when he has con-
luded that subject, he often finds that he is
bliged to return by the very same ground
iat he has just before galloped over. This
iakes his speaking often tedious; but I ad-
lit that he has acuteness: the defect I have
oticed arises out of it: he seizes a point with
ıpidity and enforces it, when he feels it
rongly, with corresponding clearness, bar-
ng a want of compression and succinct-
ɔss, which of course must detract from the
ırce of his reasoning. It seems as if he
ished to advert to all parts of a subject at
nce, from a feeling that each fact has some
earing upon another, which it is fit at the
istant to explain and illustrate: he wanders
om one end of his brief to another without

rule, order, or measure, but be never himself appears confused or confounded, although he may succeed in confusing and confounding his hearers, who are not able to follow him with equal velocity, as they are not like him intimately acquainted with the particulars in his instructions. In this respect there can scarcely be a stronger contrast than between Sir Robert Gifford and the subject of the present article; the one is brevity, point, and proportion—the other dilation, looseness, and irregularity; the one keeps a distinct line between facts and arguments—the other jumbles both in one mass, without reference to time or place: in short, the one has a clear logical head, while the other is almost destitute of the reasoning faculty, considered as a system and a science. It has been said, that the difference between logic and wit is this that the first makes and the last confound distinctions: if confounding distinctions would prove Mr. WETHERELL to be a wit, he undoubtedly may lay just claim to that character.

He is indisputably an able lawyer as far as
nowledge is concerned, but the deficiency
 which I have spoken must of course have
 influence here : he may be a great reader
 decided cases, and may have a memory
te a common-place-book of marginal notes;
it without the power to make and perceive
ce distinctions between one and another, they
nnot be of the same utility : yet it is but fair
 allow, that I know men who differ from
e in this respect, or at least hold, that Mr.
WETHERELL possesses a considerable portion
 subtlety.   I think however that they make
me confusion between two things quite dis-
nct, subtlety and ingenuity; it is very easy
r a man to be extremely ingenious without
ny pretension to subtlety or refinement.   The
nowledge possessed by Mr. WETHERELL
 also generally very applicable: he can
lways lay his hands upon the tools with
hich he intends to work, and this is a
nalification seldom attained without great
ractice; it often happens, as in instances I
ould point out in this Court if necessary,
nat no labour, however unremitting, will

communicate it to some men of considerable learning but of dull comprehension. *Scire tuum nihil est, nisi te scire hoc sciet alter,* are the words of the proverb, and Mr. WE-THERELL takes good care that his candle shall not be hidden under a bushel; he is certainly fond of display, and avails himself of every opportunity of making his attainments, upon many subjects independent of the law, pass for quite as much or more than they are worth. It is obvious that he has a very good opinion of himself, and is anxious that others should participate in it. His appearance is certainly not in his favour, yet a very short acquaintance would convince an attentive observer that Mr. WETHERELL is by no means destitute even of personal vanity.

He came into Parliament for some Borough at the time when the Vice-Chancellor's Bill was under discussion: he made three or four long speeches upon that question, and affords one more instance of the total unfitness of most lawyers for the situation he occupied.

MR. SERGEANT BOSANQUET

AND

MR. RICHARDSON.*

Je refuse d'un cœur la vaste complaisance
Qui ne fait de mérite aucune différence.

Moliere. Misanthr. A 1

In consequence of the resignation of the Chie
Justices of the Courts of King's Bench and
Common Pleas, it is the general understanding at the Bar, that it is the intention o
Ministers to make one or both of the gentlemen, whose names stand at the head of the
present article, Puisne Judges: as this distinction is likely to be soon conferred, I have
taken an earlier opportunity of noticing them
than I should otherwise have done, in orde
that a fair opinion may be formed of thei

* The period when this article was written is suffici
ently explained in it. Some of the changes alluded t
have since been made.

qualifications for the office before their elevation to it. To criticise them when upon the Bench, to say no more of it, would be out of my province.

I cannot perhaps chuse a better time than the present for alluding to what has been considered by some (whether justly or not is another question) rather a new mode of keeping up the influence of the Crown and its advisers, as much as possible, in all departments of the profession of the Law. Until very lately it was the general notion, that after a man had attained a certain standing at the Bar, he had a sort of right to be made a Sergeant, if he thought fit to put in his claim, either from motives of precedence in his pursuit, or of station in his intercourse with the world. A Counsel who had been a certain number of years on the hinder rows of the Court of King's Bench, when an advantageous opportunity presented itself by the death of a leader on the circuit, might wish to obtain a rank which would give him a chance of succeeding to the vacancy; or having long acted as junior, and fancying

that he was qualified in other respects, h
might be ambitious of a coif, to be able t
display his qualifications as a senior: unde
such circumstances, upon application, for
merly it was understood that the grant wa
made as a matter of course.   Within a ver
recent period, however, it is stated that th
practice has been changed; that at presen
the individual or individuals in whom i
vested the power of conferring, may and d
exercise a discretion on the subject nearly in
the same way as in the case of an application
for a silk-gown.   If so, I do not say that it is
but that it may be, converted into another en-
gine for extending ministerial influence ; anc
a young man who is called to the Bar may
have another motive, in addition to all those
at present powerfully operating, for speaking
respectfully of persons in high office, and of
doing his utmost to conciliate their favour.
If this be the purpose, it is not easy to see
where the system will end : it may proceed
still lower, even to induce the Benchers of the
different Inns of Court not to recommend to
the Society any individual who wishes to be

:alled, but who in any way has rendered iimself obnoxious to the higher powers. It would be difficult, however, I apprehend, to oring this about, for many of the persons who are the seniors in these Societies, and in whom at present rests acquiescence or refusal, ire men who have either never engaged in the arduous occupations of the law, or who, having gone through its labours, have arrived at the highest rank they will ever attain: both these classes are generally above or beyond the influence of ministerial instruction.*

These remarks do not in any way touch Mr. Sergeant BOSANQUET: I think he has been advanced to the dignity of the coif about five or six years; or supposing the strictness to which I referred had been exercised even at that time, which was not the case, it would not probably have been extended to him: his

* I have since heard that I am mistaken in the supposition that coifs have been with-held: of course I shall be happy to be convinced that I am in error, but as the contradiction was given by persons in some degree interested, I am not yet satisfied.

connexion with some of the wealthiest and most powerful families in the city, independent of his own inoffensive political tenets, would have been certain to have succeeded in removing all sorts of obstacles that might oppose the promotion of many others. I believe that his principal object in being made a Sergeant was that he might hold the office of one of the leading Advocates of the Bank of England : at least, if I am not mistaken, he was appointed to the vacancy very soon after the acquisition of his new distinction. Whether the object were that he should not interfere with the business of his seniors on the circuit, or that he might be upon the spot to give his advice to the Establishment from which he received his nomination, it is certain that there was a distinct understanding that he should then give up his country practice : this sacrifice however was by no means very considerable, and he received on the other hand more than a full equivalent.

His abilities certainly come under the general denomination of respectable, and I ap-

Y

prehend that his attainments as a Lawyer are much of the same order: there is nothing very peculiar either about the one or the other, and probably he would not have obtained the situation he at present holds, (which has chiefly contributed to bring him before the public eye,) without the assistance of that family alliance of which I before spoke. The Bank prosecutions have however so rapidly multiplied of late years, that his aid in public as leading Counsel for the prosecution has often been required; he has thus become better known to the world than he would have been had his office continued as much of a sinecure as that of Sir A. Piggot, who is also retained by the Bank of England, but is the senior. I do not think that trials of this kind could be much better conducted than at present by Mr. Sergeant BOSANQUET; but they have now become almost matters of course, and he has so often gone over the same ground that his exertions are nearly mechanical. On this account the newspapers have become tired of reporting speeches, to which it would be scarcely possible for the greatest ingenuity

to give variety, and the public has almost
ceased to take an interest in such proceedings,
excepting so far as they are connected with
the great question of crimes and punishments.
For this reason, though the immense number
of prosecutions he has advised, in his capacity
of Counsel to the Bank, have been extremely
profitable to him from the fees he has received
in the progress of each, yet they have not
brought him into public notice as much as
half the quantity of business would have done,
had it been of a different kind; yet to that,
as I have said, he is principally indebted
for such acquaintance as unprofessional persons have of him. His stile of speaking has
nothing at all remarkable about it, but that
perspicuity which will, almost of course, be
found in the addresses of a man of sense, and
a staidness of delivery which sometimes renders even the narration of interesting facts
rather too somniferous.

Notwithstanding he has no commanding
talent, and although his knowledge of the law
(upon which point I speak with more hesita-

tion) may not be very extensive or deep-laid,
I still think that he will make by no means a
bad judge:* in this respect I am guided by
experience, for he has more than once presided on the circuit, in the absence of one
of the judges, from illness or some other cause.
On these occasions, he has always conducted
himself to the unanimous satisfaction of the
Bar, and though part of their approbation
may have arisen from his gentlemanly and
diffident deportment in a situation of embar-
rassment and novelty, yet it would be very
unfair not to add, that his decisions as *nisi
prius*, on points of law, if subsequently ques-
tioned, were generally sanctioned by the opinion of the Court. In fact a sound discretion
usually regulates the conduct of Mr. Sergeant
BOSANQUET: he is besides cool and deliberate in his manner, and the equality of his
temper does not seem easily disturbed. His
appearance, if that may be taken into account,

---

* Those in whom the appointment rested thought that
Mr. Sergeant Best, the subject of a preceding article,
would make a better; or at least that there were better
reasons for appointing him than Mr. Serg. BOSANQUET.

is also extremely judicial, and the perspicuity which marks his speeches at the Bar, is peculiarly important in the summing up from the Bench.

Regarding Mr. RICHARDSON I have already inserted a few sentences in a preceding article, and it would be difficult to say much more than a few sentences about him : I observed, that he was employed under the present Attorney and Solicitor-General to go through a great part of the labour of their offices, for a comparatively small part of the remuneration, and that he was therefore known in the profession by the *nick*-name of the *Devil;* I added, that the individual who filled this subordinate office usually went through the drudgery under a sort of implied promise, that if he were zealous in the cause, and rendered himself useful to his employers, when he was no longer wanted he should be converted into a Puisne Judge. This promise is now about to be fulfilled,* and it cannot

* He has since been raised to the Bench, and is now one of the Judges of the Court of Common Pleas.

be denied, as far as his conduct has appeared before the public, that he has discharged his duty with great industry and devotedness. That he is a man of learning and experience is, I believe, equally incontrovertible; but his is nearly all—this is almost the utmost praise he can obtain, even from his warmest friends, unless indeed they add a certain portion of legal acuteness, independent of quickness, and not amounting to subtlety. He has not one spark of eloquence—indeed his voice and manner are both unfortunate—the one is asthmatic, and the other spasmodic; but if he had possessed physical powers for distinguishing himself as an orator, he never could have added to his reputation in this respect. He is a mere lawyer, though more deeply read than a good many of his rivals in this heavy and entangled walk of the profession. There are some men at the Bar, who, if they have degenerated from unavoidable necessity,—the compulsion of circumstances,—into fags and drudges, came to the Bar with some expectation of gratifying laudable ambition by the display of popular talents; who have previously gained distin-

guished honours at the University, for the
ardour and success with which they entered
into the pursuit of elegant literature, and have
been admired for the ready and persuasive
eloquence they displayed at an earlier period
of their lives. Such, for instance, I believe,
is Mr. Frederick Pollock, who, if a favourable opportunity were afforded, would still
in all probability shew that he possessed very
different, not to say more admirable talents,
than those for which credit is now given him,
as a shrewd and industrious pleader; but such
undoubtedly is not Mr. RICHARDSON, who, if
it be fair to judge of his youth by his more
advanced age and by the opinion of those
who have long known him, seems never to
have had any desire to be more or better than
he is; and he will most likely soon reach the
topmost height to which his hopes and wishes
have aspired.

Excepting as I have seen him in public, I
know nothing of him : of his attainments out
of his profession I am therefore not very competent to speak : he seems to be a very mild,
gentlemanly, unassuming man, reluctant to

give offence to any body, and especially to
the members of the Court. If, devoting himself entirely to the laborious part of the profession, it cannot be said of him that

> ——————————— " his delights
> Are dolphin-like ; they shew his back above
> The element he lives in ;"

at least it cannot be complained, that, like
Mr. Raine, he displays only its inferior ex-
tremity in bad puns and coarse jokes.

NOTE.—As my object is to make these articles the
vehicles of fair but free opinion, and as what I said
respecting Messrs. E. Lawes, Holt, Rigby, and Starkie,
has been in some degree misunderstood, I subjoin the
present note to explain, that in stating that on the
trial of *Watson* they did nothing but take laborious
notes, I did not intend to imply that they could or ought
to have done more: in fact it was out of their power ;
the prisoners for whom they were counsel were not tried,
as the verdict in favour of *Watson* was followed by the
acquittal of *Thistlewood, Preston,* and *Hooper,* by consent
of the Crown. Mr. E. Lawes is a man of acuteness,
though he may now and then be much too positive in
insisting that he sees a point more clearly than other
people.——Mr. Holt is undoubtedly a cunning shrewd man,
and gave one proof of it by dedicating a book to Lord
Ellenborough.   Mr. Rigby also bears the reputation
among his friends of possessing talents ; and Mr. Starkie,
I have reason to think, is an industrious advocate and a
good lawyer. What I meant to be understood, and what
I still say, is, that I do not consider any of them equal
to the great task they then undertook.

MR. BROUGHAM.

———————Tell not me of times or danger thus !
To do a villany is dangerous ;
But in an honest action my heart knows
No more of fear than dead men do of blows :
And to be slave to times is worse to me
Than to be that which most men fear to be.

G. Withers' Motto.

IT may be said, that in order to arrive at th
subject of the present article I have passe
over many individuals, who, in point of seni
ority at least, might claim precedence—that i
I step behind the Bar, I am encountered b
Messrs. Lawes, Barrow, and many others
who being omitted, may think they have som
reason to complain of neglect: as however
am influenced not merely by the claims o
rank and standing, but by those of talent an
acquirement, those gentlemen perhaps ma
have more reason to rejoice, that though oc-

cupying the front row in Court, as far as these articles are concerned, I have let them remain in the back ground. Undoubtedly they are men of great respectability in their line, but I am not aware that they deserve any particular remark—or, in other words, that any thing I could say regarding them and their practice would materially illustrate the subject upon which I am engaged: not that I affect to be influenced solely by considerations of public utility: it is not by being useful merely that a man now-a-days, or indeed at any time, can procure and fix attention; he must often be contented with making that a secondary and least obvious purpose: " utility is not a butt at which a man may appear to take a direct aim."

The friends of those gentlemen whom I think it proper to exclude from observation may also urge, that Mr. BROUGHAM can have but little expectation to find his name among criticisms upon those who practise at the Bar; and to a certain extent they are in the right: true it is that Mr. BROUGHAM seldom makes

his appearance in any of the Courts at Westminster among men (to use the well known
words of a well known orator) *contentionis
quam veritatis cupidiores ;* but I do not know
that the quantity of business an individual
enjoys is the rule by which I should be guided in my selection, nor do I exactly see why
the notion of *the Bar* should be so narrowed:
undoubtedly many more cases and causes are
heard in those Courts than elsewhere, but they
are often, almost always, of much less importance than such as are discussed and decided
before the two great Courts of Appeal, the
Privy Council and the House of Lords : here,
too, the business is more profitable ; and as
Mr. BROUGHAM, from the nature of his other
engagements, both parliamentary and private,
cannot give that close attendance in the King's
Bench which is necessary for successful practice, he prudently confines his principal attention to them : in the Cockpit he is often
employed, and in the House of Lords, when
the Lord Chancellor sits there, his attendance
is almost daily. Surely such occupations
(independent of his representative character

which in an article like the present is inevitably coupled with his legal capacity) are much more worthy of criticism and remark, than paltry motions for rules to shew cause upon points of practice, or formal references to the Master. In cases of real magnitude, however, Mr. BROUGHAM does not refuse his presence and assistance in the Court of King's Bench; and not many terms ago he sought, through the authority of their Lordships, to compel the Bank of England to render some account of its unknown and enormous profits—profits not merely derived from the pockets, but made out of the lives, of the subjects of the country, as was indisputably established in a late Session of Parliament. In fact, on trifling occasions it is not worth his while to appear; nor is it to be denied, that from his little acquaintance with the technical routine of business, most of the industrious note-taking juniors of the back-rows would be more compeent. I do not apprehend that any applause is due to him on the score of an accurate acquaintance with the fee-multiplying intricacies of *Tidd's Practice.*

If a knowledge of these matters constitute a Lawyer, (and in the more modern acceptation of the word perhaps it does) Mr. BROUGHAM has but little right to that title: I believe he is about the last man who would wish to make any pretentions to it : he is an able and zealous Advocate, learned in the first principles and foundations of jurisprudence, in the spirit in which laws originated, the purposes for which they were established, the disadvantages that have resulted from them, the corruptions that have since crept into them ; and he is better acquainted with the mind than with the body of the law—with the spirit than with the substance ; and all unimportant details he rejects as matters partly introduced by Lawyers for pecuniary objects, to make the subject as unintelligible as possible, and partly the effect of time and altered circumstances. Yet where details are necessary to the comprehending of a particular topic, the labour he bestows upon it is unceasing, and the mass of information he collects is astonishing : still he seems never overwhelmed by it ; —he always keeps steadily in his eye the obect to which he ought to direct his inquiries, and all he obtains in his researches is adapted by him to its proper situation. He is almost the only man I ever heard of, perhaps the only man at the Bar, who is at the same time capable of taking the most enlarged view of any question, and investigating, when necessary, its most involved *minutiæ*, producing order and consistency out of apparent confusion and discordance. There are very few men, and now unhappily still fewer Lawyers, who enjoy that expansion of mind which can look at a wide subject, in all its bearings,— as if it were laid down in a sort of intellectual map before them, with its boundaries and relations. There are a thousand beings in the profession who seem born only to become and continue drudges, who grope in the dark and sometimes bring to light what they do not understand the use of, but what others comprehend and apply; but Mr. BROUGHAM stands alone pre-eminent as a man who includes in himself the most valuable of these qualifications—his intellect is capable of embracing the most expanded subject—his industry is competent to the examination of its most obscure particulars—and his acuteness and judgment enable him to refer to its best use and proper place every particle of information he acquires. There seems no task too difficult for his ardour to attempt, and he always appears more animated by the glory of success than deterred by the disgrace of failure: obstacles that would appal others, animate his exertions — urge him forward, and inspire him with additional powers and energies—with an undaunted resolution to overcome and accomplish: he seems

——————— a spirit that on life's rough sea
Loves to have his sails fill'd with a lusty wind,
Even till his sail-yards tremble, his masts crack,
And his rapt ship run on her side so low
That she drinks water and her keel ploughs air.
G. Chapman's Byron's Consp. A. 4.

Such, if I may use the expression, is Mr. BROUGHAM in theory; but I am quite ready to allow, that he is by no means all this in practice on every occasion. His labours, as an Advocate, are marked by great ability, much knowledge, and a strong and laudable

z 2

anxiety in favour of the party for whom he is engaged. I believe that few suitors, who from time to time have employed him, have had good reason to complain that he neglected their interests, or amid his numerous avocations, that he did not use his utmost exertions, whether of study or argument, in their favour.—I do not consider him so close a reasoner as many of his professional opponents; but he is distinct in his statements, acute in his observations, and generally sure in his conclusions: if he now and then wander a little from the strict line of discussion, it is seldom without some result, which leaves little reason to regret that he travelled out of his course.   The matters upon which he is usually engaged in his professional capacity, the place where they are considered, and the persons before whom they are discussed, preclude almost the possibility of displaying more talent than men of less talent than Mr. BROUGHAM possess.—In questions relating to the law of Scotland, I am informed that his opinion is looked up to by high authorities with great respect.

Mr. BROUGHAM's parliamentary is not perhaps, quite so distinct from his professiona character as could be wished; or, to speal more plainly, he is rather too much of a law yer in a place from which I should wish to se all mere lawyers excluded. What I meai will be readily understood by those who re collect the prefatory remarks I made in th criticism upon Mr. Sergeant Copley to ex plain why instances were so rare, in whicl men brought up to the law, and obtaining considerable share of business, were successfu as speakers in the Houses of Commons o Lords. It is true, that much of what I thei said will apply less to Mr. BROUGHAM thai to the Learned Gentleman whose qualifica tions were then under discussion, because ii the technical sense of the word, the former i less of a lawyer than the latter; and what is perhaps, more important, he has had little o nothing to do with *Nisi Prius* practice. I may seem strange to many, but it is not les: true, that there are scarcely any two thing: more distinct, than the speech of an advocat to a jury, and the speech of a representativ

n parliament ;—they have probably little
nore in common than the continuous flow of
anguage and the purpose of persuasion : the
neans by which the end is to be attained are
rery dissimilar. I do not intend again to
:nter into this subject, which I before tolera-
ıly fully discussed, and I only recur to it to
nake more intelligible what I wish to be un-
lerstood, when I say, that Mr. BROUGHAM
is too much of a Lawyer in Parliament : he
wanders about too much in search of objections to what he is urging ; he takes pains to
:onjure up what, perhaps, but for his ingenuity would not have been produced against
him ; he furnishes his antagonists with weapons instead of driving right on to the end of
his subject, and illustrating and enforcing it
by every auxiliary circumstance. If an objection be obvious, it may be well to remove
the apparent obstacle ; but when a plain road
is open, it is idle to desert it for the sake of
scrambling over hedges and ditches.

It is on this account principally that I am
by no means an admirer of the mode in which

Mr. BROUGHAM brings forward a great subject in a set speech, after long study and de-
liberation : it has a great deal too much of the
Edinburgh Review about it :——not that I wish
to speak slightingly of that, perhaps, incom-
parable production in its kind, but I wish to
shew that there ought to be a great difference
between a sort of *exposée* of a whole subject
in the pages of that miscellany, and a speech
in the House of Commons to a popular assembly, and through that assembly to the
whole nation.   That his harangues upon such
occasions are infinitely laboured in the matter,
I readily allow ; that he goes not only to the
bottom of a subject, but examines it on all
sides " with a most learned spirit of human
dealing," I have already stated ; but independently of the objection that it may be too
learned and too laboured for the occasion
(which may fairly admit of dispute), I say
that he weakens himself and his argument, and
fatigues even his most willing hearers, by
doing much more than is necessary.   It i
true, that after a long debate the House i
generally too impatient, to listen to the mos

avoured speaker in what is termed the reply
or the summing up of the mover, and it may
be urged, that Mr. BROUGHAM is anxious to
give at once and in one view his own arguments, the points that will be advanced in
opposition to them, and his refutation of those
points.   This may be so; but still the proceeding is injudicious, and he should recollect,
that he is not the only Member in the House
who is likely to support that side of the question: his practice in the profession might
have taught him, that an Advocate will gene-
ally, from motives of prudence, leave something to his junior, without tiring the Court
by requiring it to listen only to one Counsel
on one side, who will speak at such length as
to exhaust both his subject and his auditors.
On occasions like these to which I refer, Mr.
BROUGHAM engrosses the whole debate: it is
too much to require any set of men to listen
unceasingly to a single voice for four, five,
and six hours, in succession.

I confess that I think he is never heard to
such advantage as in reply, and especially in

reply to the flimsy flippancies of Mr.Canning:
it is quite heart-rejoicing to see him turn upon
his back this bodiless porcupine, who has all
his life been darting a venomous quill at every
party that would not patronize him: no
man does it so well or so effectually as Mr.
BROUGHAM; and Mr. Canning knows it, and
fears it: he always endeavours to postpone
speaking until Mr. BROUGHAM has been
heard, and then he runs riot in the insolence
of his uncontrouled self-sufficiency. Every
recent Session has afforded several instances
in point; and on one occasion I well remember Mr. Canning made a formal complaint to
the House, that Mr. BROUGHAM could so
seldom be drawn from "his lurking place'
until after he (Mr. Canning) had risen.

The chief characteristic of Mr. BROUG-
HAM's stile of speaking is nervous energy
he aims at little refinement: he would rathe
say a thing in a strong than in an elegan
way; and to make himself distinctly intelligible, does not scruple sometimes to utte
acknowledged vulgarisms: he takes no pain
about the formation of his periods; and if hi

expressions are well chosen and well adapted, he is more indebted to the inspiration of the subject, than to previous and deliberate purpose. 1 do not think that his eloquence ever goes much beyond the forcible and the argumentative; and though, when he was a younger man, I have once or twice known him attempt to wind up an harangue by a studied peroration, I cannot say that he was successful; and his early abandonment of the practice, shews that his persuasion was the same. His stile of address is therefore peculiarly adapted to replies, and his memory appears so tenacious, that he has little need of notes to prompt him either with the arguments on the other side, or with the answers he intends to give them.

His voice and manner are not the happiest: the first is capable of musical intonation, but he neglects all art, and often very impoliticly commences in so high a key, that he is exhausted before he arrives at his conclusion: many men, who are not gifted with lungs so strong, would be worn out long before. His action is unvaried, and not by any means well calculated to add to the force of what he is urging : he sways both arms in the same direction and at the same time, and if he happen by accident to place his hat under one of them, it is a considerable relief to the eye.

There is one suggestion I would offer with diffidence in conclusion, chiefly because I wish Mr. BROUGHAM to lose none of his impressiveness in the House, of his influence in the country ; and that is that he should not allow himself so frequently to be roused to take part in a debate.* I know that with a man of strong feelings this self command and restraint is a matter of difficult attainment, especially with so many provocatives on the one side, and so few members, from recent calamities, capable of speaking with much effect on the other. Had I adverted to this subject before the last Session, I should probably also have suggested, that he should shorten his addresses by judicious compression.

* This fault Mr. BROUGHAM corrected in the last Session—perhaps he went too much into the contrary extreme.

MR. HART AND MR. BELL.

Ben siele accoppiati, io giurerei.
Ariosto, O. F. C. 20.

No person, though little acquainted with the difference in the nature of the business transacted in our Courts of Law and Equity, could fail to be struck almost at first sight with a remarkable difference, especially in the countenances, of the practisers in the one and in the other. In the King's Bench, taking that as an example of the first, if there be a number of heavy lifeless plodders, the majority of the Counsel attending have at least an appearance of quickness and shrewdness—a vivacity and a sparkling animation, not unfrequently artificial and assumed, but most commonly aided or produced by the kind of proceeding in which they may be engaged, or of which

A a

they may be spectators. Setting aside the variety of questions occupying the Judges in term-time, the trials at *Nisi Prius*, in which so many curious and entertaining facts are developed, keep the mind alive and the faculties in a state of activity: the *vivâ voce* examinations of witnesses, where something new either of manner or conduct is offered in every stage, and the readiness that is required and displayed by Advocates in managing them, is of itself sufficient to account for the difference: the expression given to the face on such occasions in time becomes fixed and habitual.

In Chancery, the effect follows the cause just in the same way, and men look dry and dull because the business of the Court is ordinarily dry and dull also: the faces of the Counsel here possess quite a different character: some of them have " the strong lines of thought" sufficiently marked, but there is nearly a total absence of life, spirit, and energy, as if " Dulness o'er all possess'd her ancient reign," and that with full consent and approbation: many keep their features even

in stiffer buckle than their wigs; and if they
have no business (which not a few of those
that look most sagaciously have not) with their
senses scarcely awake, yet, with their eyes
open, they preserve all day a sort of listening
attitude with a blind pertinacity almost equal
to that of an Indian Faquir; — "list'ning they
hear not, looking they not see." Whether a
cause be or be not proceeding, whether a
Counsel be or be not speaking, they "still sit
fixed to hear" with a most solemn gaze of un
thinking investigation; as if striving to look
wise with all their might, the exertion had
been so great as to send them off in a sort o
half doze, or, like a sober man, ashamed o
being a little tipsy, using every effort to com
mand his relaxed features, and to call up a
look of uncommon thoughtfulness.—Though
elbowing each other for hours, they seldom
converse: a hearty joke in Chancery would
be something like the *coup-de-main* in th
Scheldt which Lord Chatham was to execute
and which Windham so successfully ridicul
ed : such a thing is never heard, or if it wer
hazarded, the Barristers would either not b

A a 2

sufficiently awake to comprehend it, or would meet it only by a smile of compassionate surprise. Now and then indeed the Lord Chancellor may "make a sun-shine in a shady place," by launching a pun, but the illumination is only partial; it reaches the Solicitors and the Suitors, and sets them giggling, but very rarely produces an enlivening effect upon the solemn rows of wigs and gowns.

As I have said, this sombre appearance is occasioned chiefly by the nature of the business in which the Counsel in Chancery are engaged.—I recollect once hearing a lady, (for ladies are the best judges of these matters) on entering the Court for the first time, remark, " Dear me, what a set of ill-looking men they are;" and it was true of them as a whole, though of course there are exceptions; the hollow cheeks, sunken eyes, and unrefreshed complexions of many of the Barristers, sufficiently show the unalleviated laboriousness of their occupations, particularly out of Court. Of fifty or sixty Counsel who devote themselves publicly to the profession in Chan-

cery, I scarcely know of more than one com
plete exception, and he, with a great deal
business, and necessarily a close attention
it, still preserves much of the external, if n
internal, freshness of the flower whose nan
he bears. If Mr. HART in some degree keep
up appearances in this particular, he is i
debted for his swarthy complexion to h
West Indian birth and originally oriental e:
traction. Mr BELL is corpulent, but it is le
attributable to health than to sedentary en
ployments.

With regard to the acquirements and qu
lifications of these two gentlemen, it seems
me that they are pretty nearly matche
excepting that the manner of Mr. HART
superior to that of Mr. BELL: the latter is
north-countryman, and in every way seen
through life to have disdained all kind
polish or refinement: his brogue is, I appr
hend, quite as strong now as when he first le
his native country; and I am not at all su
that of late it has not been of some service
him, and that, if it had been possible, it wou

not have been extremely impolitic in him to have corrected it. It is a common remark, that a man's enemies sometimes turn out to be his best friends, and this is the case with Mr. BELL's provincial accent: it might be an obstruction to his progress when a younger man, but of late years he has built his reputation and his fortune very much upon it; for in a Court like the Chancery, where so little depends, as I have before explained, upon externals, suitors immediately conclude that a man who is so defective in voice, manner and pronunciation, must be an admirable Lawyer; that he will have taken great pains in one way to countervail such serious obstacles in another. There are not many men now at the Bar who recollect "honest Jack Lee" (as he was familiarly called, principally on account of his coarse straight-forward bluntness,) but I am told by those who do, that he had the same northern brogue as Mr BELL, and that he gained a great deal of his extensive practice in the same way, by obtaining a character for being a good Lawyer, because, popularly speaking, he was a bad Advocate. There is not the least doubt, however, that Mr. BELL merits much of what is attributed to him upon this score; and there is not a man who knows him, from the Barrister to the Chancellor himself, who does not look up to his opinions, particularly upon ecclesiastical matters, with the utmost respect.——" Equity (says Selden in his most, or rather his only, popular work) is a roguish thing: for the Law we have a measure, we know what to trust to; Equity is according to the conscience of him that is Chancellor, and as that is larger or narrower, so is Equity. 'Tis all one as if they should make the standard for measure a Chancellor's foot: what an uncertain measure would this be. One Chancellor has a long foot, another a short foot, a third an indifferent foot: 'tis the same thing in the Chancellor's conscience."——Most likely, Lord Eldon has this sentence, or at least this sentiment, impressed upon his mind, and it occasions the dilatoriness of which parties, Counsel, Suitors, Solicitors, and even the Judge himself complains;—but it is not a little increased when his Lordship knows that Mr. BELL's opinion is in opposition to that which he himself has adopted. To state it, however, is not such high praise to Mr. BELL as might be imagined, for he is by no means singular in this particular. There can scarcely be a greater misfortune connected with the administration of justice, than for a Chancellor (a man placing himself in a situation where he is called upon to determine, and for which by taking the office he declares himself in his own judgment competent) to have no opinion of his own, and to prefer that of the Advocate whose business it is to endeavour to mislead him.

Mr. BELL is a remarkable instance of success in spite of an absence of all those qualifications usually considered requisite in an Advocate, except industry, and a memory of peculiar retentiveness. Independent of his broad accent, he is a very hesitating speaker, and has sometimes great difficulty in making himself intelligible : it is generally said, setting diffidence aside, that what a man sees clearly he can state clearly ; but I think Mr. BELL is an exception ; for he has a good deal

of subtelty in drawing distinctions, but is
totally deficient in all facility of explaining
them. He is however extremely patient and
persevering, and will not object, whatever
may be the wishes of his hearers, to go over
the same point again and again, until he
thinks he is distinctly understood.

Mr. HART is also what is termed a very
sound Equity Counsel, and besides his public
practice has, like Mr. BELL, a great quantity of Chamber business, or cases to be answered. He has certainly a much better voice
and manner than Mr. BELL, for at least there
is nothing about them that is offensive and
displeasing to the ear or eye. Mr. HART,
however, is a dull man—a mere plodder in
old beaten tracks, where he has most merit
who can remember most of the way he has
gone. I do not say that he wants shrewdness,
but he most assuredly wants intelligence, and
on this account I do not consider him by any
means a good reasoner. His chief merit, independent of his knowledge, seems to me to
lie in this,—that he can state the facts of an

interwoven and entangled case with tolerable perspicuity ; but in this there is a great deal that is merely mechanical, and applause may as frequently be due to the Solicitor who instructs him, as to the Advocate, who perhaps only simply states the circumstances in the order in which they have been detailed in his brief. Upon this point, therefore, it is sometimes difficult to settle the *quantum meruit* of praise: it is but a second or perhaps a third-rate faculty at last, unless it be accompanied with that ingenious location of facts, for which the present Attorney-General is so distinguished, and which, without more, is of itself an argument on the side of the case he supports.

Mr. HART is fluent but never forcible. I never heard him utter an eloquent sentence even by accident: all he aims at is a regular conversational mode of doing business, by which he travels over his ground quickly, and thereby renders his practice as profitable as other circumstances will allow.

MR. NOLAN, MR. GASELEE,
MR. CASBERD, MR. WARREN
MR. HARRISON.

If reason in man were of equal weight with his pride he could never be pleased with praises which he is conscious he don't deserve.——Mandeville's Fab. of the Bees.

In the present article it is my intention to speak of the Counsel with silk gowns in the Court of King's Bench, whose names and qualifications I have not hitherto mentioned. I give Messrs. NOLAN, GASELEE, and CASBERD, a presedence here, which they are not entitled to elsewhere, because as they have been recently appointed, and their advancement in consequence inserted in the newspapers, they are perhaps better known to the public than Messrs. WARREN and HARRISON, who are of considerably longer standing before the Bar.

Without meaning to say any thing unneces-
arily unhandsome, I really am quite at a loss
o conjecture for what reason Mr. NOLAN has
)een nominated one of his Majesty's Counsel
earned in the law : in general that situation
1as been obtained either by commanding
alents or commanding influence, but most
:ommonly by the latter : of this I am well
:onvinced, that though the individual in
]uestion may be a very good natured, well-in-
tentioned man, with a competent share of
professional knowledge, he has few other qualifications to entitle him to the rank he has
attained.   If length of standing were the cri-
terion, there are several gentlemen who ought
to have been advanced before him ;   and in
learning I could point out many acknowledged
superiors who have not yet dreamt of aspiring
to such a station.   True it is, that Mr. NOLAN
has written, or rather edited, a book—a book, I
am ready to allow, of authority on a particular
branch of the law ; but in this respect he is by
no means singular, though (perhaps with one
exception, and that too an exception applying
to one of the worst books ever published) if

he be indebted to it for his honours, he is singular in being the first man who ever was so
rewarded, and on such an account. There
are not a few individuals, who have printed
admirable volumes, upon many complicated
subjects connected with the administration of
justice, who have been remunerated neither
by the profits of the labours of their pens, by
increased practice, nor by sharing in any of
the honours which the Administration is capable of bestowing. What private influence
Mr. NOLAN may enjoy, it is not for me to
inquire: my business is only to ascertain, as
impartially as I can, his fitness for the situation he now holds.

I have already said that Mr. NOLAN is by
no means a man of talents in any sense in
which the word can be applied to an Advocate. His friends and admirers at the Surrey
Sessions, the Magistrates who usually preside,
and with whom he may be upon terms of social intimacy, may think that I do not fairly
estimate his powers; and it is very true that
I have but rarely seen them exercised in that

B b

situation : it is equally true, however, that I
have witnessed his practice in the Court of
King's Bench and on the circuit very frequently, and I am not aware that he ever much distinguished himself by displaying eloquence
and skill in addressing a jury, acuteness in
interrogating a witness, or readiness in meeting a point of law, and obviating an objection
of form.   I do not say that he is by any means
deficient, excepting so far as not possessing
in the rank he now fills, is deficiency; and
supposing private influence out of the question, I am at a loss how to account for his
elevation.   This was by no means the case
with Mr. Warren or Mr. Harrison, two other
King's Counsel, of whom I shall say more
presently : every body knows that the first
was connected with many Members of Parliament, and the other for a series of years
had luxuriated in the office of Counsel to the
Treasury.   I do not believe that Mr. NOLAN
had any such advantages.

The remarks I have made upon Mr. Nolan
will to a considerable extent apply to Mr.
GASELEE who has even less popular talent.

He is reckoned a very skilful pleader, a very industrious and well-informed chamber Coun sel, and a very judicious and useful junior but these are not qualifications which usually have obtained for a Barrister the distinction of a silk gown : he would perhaps have been the last man I should have named, had I been told to guess at the appointments, not merely because his attainments, and in some sort the peculiar nature of his business, seem to fit him to act in a subordinate sphere, but because I should suppose that he would be a great loser by his promotion : he must of course give up all that lucrative part of his practice which is technically called *drawing*,* and the opini ons required from him must of necessity be diminished : few will give two, four, or six guineas, for that which elsewhere they can obtain for one, two, or three. I never saw Mr GASELEE address a Jury, and very probably I never shall, for the notion I entertain of his abilities is, I believe, common among those whose good opinion it is most important for

* The word *drawing* and *to draw* is differently explained in Grose's Slang Dictionary, but it is capable of much the same application.

ιim to secure: he has neither force of lan-
;uage nor of manner to make any impression
ιs a speaker, and though upon matters of law
ιnd delicate niceties of pleading he may be
ιble to make himself very intelligible to the
Jourt, and to obtain a number of admirers of
ιis learning in decided cases, and of his sub-
lety in drawing distinctions, such qualifica-
ions, as I have often said, have little or no
:onnexion with the duties of a *Nisi Prius*
ιdvocate. The very best *Nisi Prius* Advo-
:ate that ever lived was most deficient in all
hese particulars. I admit that the business
ιf a King's Counsel is not merely to lead in
:ases before a Jury; but if he be not compeent to that, he must forego one of the most
ιrofitable parts of the profession.

Mr. CASBERD has succeeded in obtaining
ι patent of precedence, a privilege of no
nconsiderable importance, for as was ex-
ιlained before when I spoke of Mr. Jervis it
nables him to defend persons prosecuted by
he Crown for any offences, without the ne-
:essity of the licence, which is obtained for a
King's Counsel at a heavy expence to their

clients. He is eminent as a Lawyer, havin
distinguished himself on several occasion
not forgetting the great case of King v. Lor
Rivers, in which he addressed the Court :
Serjeant's Inn for, I believe, two successiv
days. But independent of his attainments i
this respect, he is by no means a bad publi
speaker, I mean in addresses to the Jury.
have had an opportunity of listening to hir
with pleasure several times on the Wester
Circuit, and if I am not much mistaken,
very considerable share of the business ther
will fall to his lot in consequence of his recer
appointment. He by no means wants fluer
cy, but he is rather deficient in impressive
ness: he is uncommonly quick without muc
of the appearance of it, for he has rather
slow, or (to use an expressive though some
what vulgar word) a drawling tone of voice
and a manner not altogether inconsistent wit
it: his countenance also has too little variety
we often see the faces of men express a grea
deal more and better than they think, but th
contrary is the case with Mr. CASBERD. II
is a Member of Parliament, but I do not re

B b 3

collect ever hearing him speak there, or seeing
his name in the newspapers excepting in lists
of *majorities*. To this circumstance, perhaps,
for I speak hesitatingly,) may be attributed
the peculiar advantage he has within a short
time obtained over his competitors.

It remains for me to notice Mr. WARREN
and Mr. HARRISON, two King's Counsel,
who have sat for some years before the Bar,
but whose names and merits are comparatively little known to the public : yet their time
has been by no means unprofitably, though
rather unostensibly, employed, for they have
enjoyed a great share of business before Committees of the House of Commons. This is
a branch of the profession to which I have
not yet had an opportunity of adverting, and
it is not by any means the least lucrative or
honourable : Counsel who are employed by
Candidates, in cases of contested elections, are
always most liberally feed ; and where the
conflict is protracted, small fortunes are made
out of the pockets of those who have large
fortunes to spend. In the same way, when

private Bills are brought into Parliament for enclosures or turnpike-roads (which, by the bye, are not unfrequently jobs between the Attornies and Surveyors of the Parish), one party promotes and another opposes the project, and the merits are in consequence referred to a select number of Members of Parliament: Counsel are employed to discuss the matter before them, and to conduct the examinations of the various witnesses, and many hundred pounds are frequently disbursed about a piece of waste land, the fee simple of which is not worth one-tenth part of the sum expended on its enclosure.

To matters like these the attention of Messrs. WARREN and HARRISON has been principally devoted: the former of these gentlemen has never laid himself out for common law business; and though the latter, at one period of his life, would willingly have obtained it, he has more recently been quite as profitably and probably less laboriously occupied in his official capacity, in perusing and settling the various Bills brought into Parliament by Ministers, independent of those which he has been employed to consider for private parties. He has besides generally obtained his share of business before Committees; and if Mr. WARREN appeared on the one side, Mr. HARRISON generally led on the other. The qualifications necessary for such a situation are pretty much those required by a *Nisi Prius* Advocate, excepting that a knowledge of the practice of Parliament and its Committees is to be substituted for an acquaintance with the rules of evidence and such technical points of law as ordinarily arise in our Courts. Mr. WARREN has obtained a considerable and a deserved reputation for his learning on the law of elections, a peculiar and in some respects an intricate branch of knowledge, and for the readiness in difficulties, as well as the general acuteness he displays when the exercise of his talent is required. Sometimes however he is charged with being a little slovenly in the manner in which he conducts business of this kind, but I must admit at the same time that it is where peculiar industry and address were not required. He is a very fluent and a perspicuous speaker, and by no means deficient in impressiveness, the powe of exciting and securing attention. The wan of this faculty is Mr. HARRISON's principa defect: no man can exceed him in volubility he perhaps utters more words in a given tim than any other man at the Bar, and to th purpose, for he seldom travels out of his case but he is the least or one of the least effectiv speakers in the profession. Mr. Adolphus i perhaps next to him in rapidity, but far be fore him in emphasis and expression: Mr HARRISON's mode of speaking is one conti nued, almost unintelligible rattle, that wearie the ear instead of attracting it. In examinin a witness however he often shews great shrewd ness and skill, though it not uncommonl happens that he is obliged to put the questio twice over, because an unpractised witnes cannot follow the velocity of his delivery Both these gentlemen probably reaped golden harvest in the last Session, in con sequence of the number of petitions presented against the return of sitting Members.—Pri vate Bills have been much less numerous fo

he last two or three years than formerly,
partly owing to the re-establishment of peace
and the absence of one great inducement to
cultivation of the soil, and partly to the
nhabitants of the country districts having
been made acquainted by dear-bought experience, with the enormous expences attendant
upon Acts of Parliament for inclosures and
other improvements.

MR. SERGEANT PELL.

" God forgive me if I slander them with the title of learned, for generally they are not."—*Nash's Lenten Stuff*, 1599.

THIS gentleman was omitted in the original series of these articles, because at the time they were written he did not seem to occupy so ostensible a station at the Bar, either in point of business or of talent, as to render it necessary to make him an object of criticism. I well remember him before he obtained the dignity of the coif, when he occupied a seat on about the third or fourth row behind the Bar, and I believe it was the astonishment of many for what reason he had sought this advancement; he was then in possession of a share of practice, though small, and circumstances seemed to promise that by the change he would lose even that.

Of course it was impossible to enter into his private motives and speculations, and whatever they were they seem by no means to have failed. Yet I cannot persuade myself, that he ever contemplated the good fortune he has experienced. At present no man possesses more extensive business on the western circuit than Mr. Sergeant PELL; he may be said to lead on one side or on the other in almost every cause, and in small matters I am far from thinking that he does not give satisfaction to his clients; in great matters, country reverence often carries men in their admiration far beyond their judgments; that is to say again, what has been said a thousand times before, they admire what they cannot understand—they " wonder with a foolish face of praise," and commonly measure the merit of a speech by the length of time it has occupied in the delivery.

My reason for believing that Mr. Sergeant PELL could scarcely have contemplated the good fortune he has experienced on his circuit is this, that when first he went it in the

acquired rank of a senior and with the pre
tensions of a leader, the higher places wei
occupied by such men as Sir V. Gibbs an
Mr. Sergeant Lens, and others were graduall
rising into notice and favour: those two ir
dividuals however nearly monopolized all th
leading business, and it was obvious to a
who knew any thing upon the subject, tha
Sir R. Gifford must in a short time occupy a
least the third station. These were apparentl
insuperable obstacles to Mr. Sergeant PELI
because he must know (for he is not without
portion of diffidence, and has acuteness enoug
to measure his own powers) that he was nc
able to compete with them, and that his onl
chance was their removal out of his way: the
have been removed; Sir V. Gibbs was create
a judge, Mr. Serjeant Lens retired from tha
part of his most extensive practice, and S:
R. Gifford was appointed solicitor-genera
and as a matter, I believe, of course, gave u
the emoluments he was accustomed to deriv
from the country, at the moment when h
was certain of obtaining as much or perhaj
more than any individual who had precede

im.   There is in fact upon the whole, often
uite as much good luck in the success of
ounsel as ability : indeed instances have been
dduced, where a few happy coincidences
ave thrown upon men of low talents and
o attainments overburdening employment,
ven in the metropolis, where the capabilities
f Barristers are generally best understood,
nd most correctly estimated.

It is perhaps not too much to say, that the
ace of Mr. Sergeant PELL has been of con-
iderable use to him.   1 have before observed
pon the sort of artificial quickness of expression which the countenances of some bar-
isters acquire, especially those who are in
he habit of attending at *nisi prius ;* besides,
ome actually assume it—it is a matter of effort
with them to look shrewd and sagacious, and
t may be fairly asserted that they put on their
aces and their wigs at the same time : this is
ιot a little aided by the peculiar shape in
which a few procure their wigs to be made—
with a cropt snugness, if I may use the word,
that looks extremely brisk and taking.   But

Mr. Sergeant PELL always had a peculiarl
lively eye, a sharp penetrating nose, and
mouth indicating more taste, and possessin
more expression than I have reason to believ
he enjoys. These to him are gifts of Nature
and perhaps in externals she may have bee
upon the whole more favourable to him tha
in other more important respects. Althoug
I used to think highly of Mr. Sergeant (no
Mr. Justice) Best as an advocate, it is not t
be denied that he owed a great deal of th
impression he made upon a jury and a
audience (for he never failed to make his ad
dresses general) to the keenness and fire c
his eye.

Though I do not feel at all warranted i
putting Mr. Sergeant PELL upon a level wit
Mr. Sergeant Best, indeed in many particu
lars they ought not be named on the sam
day, yet there is a similarity beyond the loo
of quickness and shrewdness I have men
tioned, and which does go, and ought to g
a great way in convincing people that th
possessor of that look is also the possessor c

the qualities it indicates. Mr. Sergeant PELL is unquestionably a quick shrewd man, but when this is said, I apprehend I have gone nearly to the extent of the praise I feel warranted in bestowing : yet they are two of the most useful and indispensable qualifications of a *nisi prius* advocate, and for this reason, before a jury, this gentleman is most in his sphere.

His chief excellence does not consist in his speeches either in opening a case or in replying to it : the latter are the best, but both are deficient in requisites of some importance. I should be inclined, in speaking of matters of this sort, to make a distinction between volubility and fluency; yet a speaker who is voluble can hardly be said not to be fluent; but my meaning is, that in fluency there is something included beyond mere rapidity of utterance, for it seems to convey the idea of a regular flow of a steady current still pressing forward to its end, without the varieties not inconsistent with volubility : fluency also appears to imply something of system and

proportion, while mere volubility may be
without any arrangement, and may be formed
of sentences absolutely dislocated and uncon-
nected, but at the same time delivered without any considerable interruption. Now I
apprehend that I speak correctly when I say
that Mr. Sergeant PELL is rather voluble than
fluent, and though he may be able to speak
as rapidly as any man, there is almost always
a want of order and proportion in what he
says : for this reason a complicated case can
scarcely be in worse hands, while one depend-
ing upon a few facts and circumstances can
certainly not be in much better on the circui
where he practises. In addition, there is ofter
a display of that common defect of judgment
which consists in pressing points of too little
importance : I do not mean to say that he
omits to urge those of most consequence, but
he frequently takes as much pains and bestows as much emphasis upon the former as
upon the latter : this has the effect of wearying
his auditors in some degree, and diminishes
the impressiveness and effect of his whole
speech. Formerly he had a short snappish

catching kind of delivery, but since he has had more practice, he has much overcome this defect.

As a lawyer, I am disposed by no means to rank him high, but I am not sure whether full justice is done him, because he has always been accompanied on his circuit by men of first rate eminence in this respect: three of them I have already mentioned, and at present Mr. Casberd and Mr. Gaselee will keep up its reputation even should Mr. Sergeant PELL add nothing to it. An opinion prevails in the West of England, where it is most important that such an opinion should prevail, that Mr. Sergeant PELL is an excellent counsel upon matters relating to elections. Upon this point I profess my incompetence to give a judgment, for I have never but once had an opportunity of seeing him engaged before a Committee of the House of Commons; his written opinions upon such subjects have never come under my observation, nor have I heard any competent individual speak either in praise or dispraise of them.

It is by no means difficult for any person who has seen Mr. Sergeant PELL conduct a cause only once or twice to point out his principal recommendation : it is that of most quick ready men, viz. his mode of examining a witness who is reluctant to disclose the truth He is always on the alert to catch the witness tripping, and succeeds oftener from this extreme vigilance than from any particular ingenuity in framing his questions and extracting answers. His experience is here of course of the utmost use to him.

After all, though he will never be a very eminent, he will always be a very useful counsel, and as second in the management of a cause, where he has not to address the Jury he is likely to give general satisfaction : at present however he is at the head of his circuit, and cannot be employed in the country without leading, unless a senior be brought down by the expensive process of a special retainer. In London Mr. Sergeant PELL has comparatively little business, and I doubt if it will be ever extensive.

MR. CULLEN, MR. HORNE, MR. HEALD, AND MR. WINGFIELD.

There's nothing simply good, nor ill alone ;
Of every quality comparison
The only measure is, and judge opinion.
Dr. Donne's Progr. of the Soul, St. 52

THE objects of ambition, separated from pe
cuniary consideration, are much less numero
in Chancery than in our Courts of Law, b
those who aim at the highest honours eve
in the latter are not by any means in propo
tion to the probability of attainment.   Inde
the Barristers in Westminster Hall appear
have multiplied so rapidly within the last te
or fifteen years, that in none of the Courts a
the seats assigned to them sufficient for tl
purpose.   In this respect, in the Comm

Pleas, during Term, the Advocates are least incommoded, because none but Sergeants are allowed to practise; the dreary coldness and dullness of the Exchequer usually keeps away nearly all but those who have actual business to transact. The Court of King's Bench, however, as I had occasion before to remark, is generally crowded to excess, and in Chancery, unless I am much mistaken, the proportion of Barristers attending has of late been more considerable than for many previous years. The cause of this influx is not the creation of any new offices, to which their hopes may ascend, but the great increase of business; for the love of money as every body knows is a much more generally operative impellent than the desire of rank, unless indeed the rank bring with it a proportionate pecuniary emolument. The fact of the large increase of Barristers who devote their time to Chancery practice, where strickly speaking there are but three judicial situations open to them, establishes what I have said. Sometimes indeed a common lawyer is advanced to the Woolsack and to the custody of the

Great Seal, as in the recent case of Lor
Erskine, but it more rarely happens (an
the instance of Sir James Mansfield canno
be fairly quoted to the contrary) that a mer
equity lawyer is appointed chief justice eithe
of the King's Bench or Common Pleas : the
are made *puisne* Barons and sometimes Chief
barons of the Exchequer, but I cannot recol
lect that at any period the inferior judicia
seat of the common-law courts have been fille
by individuals selected from the Chancer
Bar.

Independent of the gentlemen in bomba
sine who either practise or sit in this Court, i
is provided with no less than twelve King'
Counsel, who all enjoy either more or les
business. Six of these have already beer
under review in the course of these articles ;
one I have cursorily noticed, another I have
totally omitted, and of the four remaining
candidates for employment I am now about to
speak.

Mr. CULLEN, I apprehend, may lay claim

to the first mention on the ground of seniority if not of merit. He examines the cases entrusted to him with great care, and conducts them with much prudence: he seems faithfully to adhere to his instructions, and never commits the interests of his clients by indiscretion: he is a man perhaps of more labour than talent, who makes up for his deficiency in the latter by unabated industry, and who from reading and experience has acquired as much knowledge as most of those to whom he is usually opposed. His method is very systematic, and his manner somewhat laboured, with a mouthing kind of pronunciation that looks a little like pompous effort, where an exertion of the kind is totally unnecessary: he affects to be oratorical in the wrong place, or I should rather say that he is seldom oratorical in the right: he makes a common observation upon a matter of form with quite as much, if not more ceremony than if it were a remark upon the most pinching and important part of the case. Yet do not let me be understood to say, that he is by any means an exception to that gentlemanly deportmen

which usually prevails in the Court of Chan
cery, excepting in a deficiency of ease : he i
never frivolous in his addresses to the Chan
cellor, he wastes but little time, but proceed
to the gist of the argument, and in combattin;
it not unfrequently evinces both readiness an
ingenuity.   He is a quicker man than hi
general appearance indicates : his small blacl
eye is sharp and piercing, and it is extremel;
difficult for any thing to escape its scrutiny
His voice is not inharmonious, but it want
articulation and distinctness : perhaps th
attempt to remedy this defect has occasione
the mouthing and too apparent exertion o
the muscles of the face to which I have re
ferred.

Of Mr. HORNE I feel competent to say bu
little, because from various accidents, whicl
it would not perhaps be very easy, and cer
tainly not very necessary to explain, I hav
seldom had an opportunity of listening t
him while he has been employed in address
ing either the Chancellor, the Vice-Chancellor, or the Master of the Rolls.   All tha

I have heard and seen however has pleased me, and if I have not heard more it did not arise from the circumstance that he enjoys but little business, for the fact is directly the reverse. He seems a man of a sound understanding and of a clear head, and conducts himself without pretence of any kind. He is esteemed a good Equity Lawyer and his appearance is just the idea of a Chancery Advocate: his countenance is rather thoughtful than bright: some men make their faces mere mirrors reflecting external impressions, operated upon by the cloudyness or clearness of the weather, by the presence of particular individuals, and a thousand other circumstances; but the face of a thoughtful man is always much the same, and he is not particularly excited by what is passing within or without: this is the case with Mr. HORNE, who has gained the character with some on his account of being a heavy man. In his practice I have remarked nothing to warrant this opinion, unless a tranquil sobriety of deportment be mistaken for drowsy dulness.

The tone of his voice is something too deep
and may have a lulling sort of murmur t
those who attend the Court for the mere pur
pose of gratifying useless curiosity. I thinl
his manner at times peculiarly forcible, an
he has often, when I have seen him, an earnest
ness about his delivery that secured my at
tention.

Against the third gentleman on this list
Mr. HEALD, I can say nothing, but that t
a slighter degree he has the defect I notice
in Mr. BELL; viz. a strong northern dialect
but it is by no means of so vulgar and coars
a kind. Yet Mr. HEALD invariably forget
the aspirate where it ought to be sounded, i
he do not sometimes insert it where it ough
to be omitted. He is a straight-forwar
speaker, and would most likely as soon thinl
of returning to the North as attempting an
thing approaching an oratorical flourish
This may be considered extraordinary b
those who knew him in his youth, when
am informed that he devoted himself to th
pursuit of the *belles lettres,* and even pub

lished a poem of considerable humour on a ludicrous dispute between two Scots physicians. His face is of a fine contour, and to look at him one would not suppose that he had degenerated into a mere lawyer. He is a man of very considerable learning in his profession, and his general attainments are highly respectable. He is a very distinct and intelligible stater of a long case, and has a great facility at seizing the leading points, and reducing the whole to as narrow a compass as possible : I do not say that he equals Sir R. Gifford in this particular, for no man equals him ; but he is not behind Mr. Hart in this sort of excellence. Mr. HEALD is also a very acute and clear reasoner—he has an eye for nice shades of distinction, and can evolve a subtle fallacy with great shrewdness and dexterity. I have cause to know that his opinions as a chamber-counsel are highly esteemed.

I am sorry that the advancement of Mr. WINGFIELD to the rank of King's Counsel renders it in some degree necessary for me to

make a few observations upon him. Had h
continued behind the Bar, I should certainl;
have avoided saying any thing about him
but he could not well be omitted in an articl
devoted to Gentlemen who at the same tim
received the same distinction. Perhaps h
would prefer notice at all events to entire ex
clusion under such circumstances. As it i
much more pleasant to advert to a man'
good qualities, I will begin by admitting tha
Mr. WINGFIELD's greatest excellence is hi
quickness, but like many others destitute o
sound judgment, he thinks it is worth a grea
deal more than its real value, and that th
enjoyment of it will amply supply the plac
even of material deficiences. True it is, tha
there is a certain class who, like him, priz
it highly, and it is equally true that there ar
certain situations where the possession of mer
quickness is of considerable importance : a
advocate before a jury, for instance, is los
without it—nothing can compensate for it
absence in examining a cunning witness, or i
making a reply to a case ingeniously and
artfully fabricated : under such circumstance

a Counsel had much better be destitute of all knowledge of the principles and precedents of law than of quickness: but the Court of Chancery is a very different place, and requires very different talents and attainments. On this account, if Mr. WINGFIELD had originally begun to practise in any of our Courts of Law, I am not at all sure whether he would not have met with more success than at present he can be congratulated upon, even though he may have attained a place within the Bar. In fact, this Gentleman often conducts himself in equity too much like a *nisi prius* advocate, with much of the flippant confidence that might be very useful if he were so, but is offensive in the situation where he usually displays it, and where a calm decorum is preserved, sometimes carried to too great an extreme, but commonly well calculated for the attainment of justice in a Court where "passion wears the livery of thought," and where it is vain to make an attempt to play with the feelings or impose upon the understanding. Mr. WINGFIELD may be a better lawyer than he is, I believe,

ordinarily considered by those who take of
fence when they hear him address the Cour
with a sort of assured air, and in a tone o
voice that would indicate that he is upon mos
excellent terms with himself, and is acquaintec
with few individuals better entitled to be hearc
at any length he may deem requisite.

————————

I have now brought to a close these CRI-
TICISMS ON THE BAR : the object I had in
view I stated in the outset, and how far tha
object has been attained it is not of mucl
importance for me to inquire ; that is a poin
which can be better settled by others.   Thu:
much I will say, that they have been dictated by a spirit of candid but liberal enquiry,
and I have never intentionally wounded individual feelings, nor intruded into the privacy
of domestic life.   I have spoken of men only
as I saw them in public, figuring on the open
stage of our Courts of Justice, and whatevei
other ambition I may have indulged, I shall
be content if I have been useful.   I have

heard some objections stated to these articles upon principle, but none that could not be answered: I am not called upon to answer them here; but to those who urge that Barristers are not fit objects of public criticism—that their qualifications and conduct ought to pass without remark, I reply in the stale quotation *Quis tulerit Gracchos, &c.* Shall those who are so little sparing of their censures, and so free in their observations, complain because their merits and defects are attempted to be fairly canvassed and impartially ascertained.

FINIS.

Printed by G. HAYDEN, Little College Street, Westminster.

THE BORROWER WILL BE CHARGED
THE COST OF OVERDUE NOTIFICATION
IF THIS BOOK IS NOT RETURNED TO
THE LIBRARY ON OR BEFORE THE LAST
DATE STAMPED BELOW.

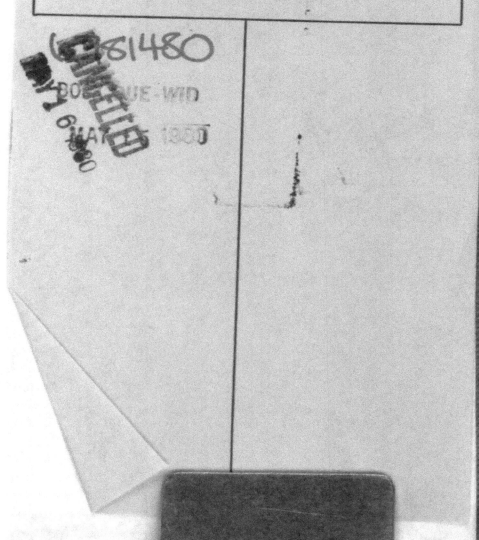